M000197740

España

España

EXPLORING
THE FLAVORS
OF SPAIN

James Campbell Caruso

photography by **Douglas Merriam**

GIBBS SMITH
TO ENRICH AND INSPIRE HUMANKIND

First Edition
16 15 14 13 12   5 4 3 2 1
Text © 2012 by James Campbell Caruso
Photographs © 2012 by Douglas Merriam

All rights reserved. No part of this book may be reproduced by
any means whatsoever without written permission from the
publisher, except brief portions quoted for purpose of review.

Published by
Gibbs Smith
P.O. Box 667
Layton, Utah 84041
1.800.835.4993 orders
www.gibbs-smith.com

Designed by Michelle Farinella Design

Printed and bound in China

Gibbs Smith books are printed on either recycled,
100% post-consumer waste, FSC-certified papers or on
paper produced from sustainable PEFC-certified forest/controlled
wood source. Learn more at www.pefc.org.

Library of Congress Cataloging-in-Publication Data

Caruso, James Campbell.
España : exploring the flavors of Spain / James Campbell Caruso ;
photographs by Douglas Merriam. — 1st ed.
p. cm.
Includes index.
ISBN 978-1-4236-2423-3
1. Cooking, Spanish. 2. Cookbooks. I. Title.
TX723.5.S7C3564 2012
641.5946—dc23
                                                            2011041616

To James William Campbell, Sr.,
1935–2001
You are still with me every day.

Also, to the people of Spain, the
entire Santa Fe Community, and
the team at La Boca Restaurant in
Santa Fe, New Mexico

Contents

Marmitako   69
Tuna and Potato Stew

Sopa de Bacalao   70
Bacalao and Potato Soup

Sopa de Mejinnoes   71
Tomato-Fennel Fish
Broth with Mussels

Vegetable Tapas

Queso de Cabra con Sofrito   74
Baked Goat Cheese with Sofrito

Alcachofas   77
Grilled Artichokes with Goat
Cheese, Orange, and Mint

Berenjenas Parrillas   78
Grilled Eggplant with
Melted Manchego, Capers,
and Saffron Honey

Aguacates con Roncal   79
Avocados with Shaved
Roncal and Olive Oil

Alcaparonnes   80
Fried Caperberries

Escalivada   83
Roasted Vegetables

Esparrogos Olivada   84
Grilled Asparagus with Olivada

Esparragos Blancos   85
White Asparagus in Sherry
Vinaigrette, Oranges, and Parsley

Revueltos   86
Scrambled Eggs with Asparagus
and Manchego on Toasts

Cazuela de Espinaca   89
Baked Spinach with Goat Cheese
and Onion-Raisin Compota

Pincho de Huevo   90
Egg Bruschetta with
Mushrooms and Truffle Oil

Betabeles   92
Roasted Beets

Alborina   93
Roasted Autumn Vegetables
and Peppers

Manchego Frito   95
Fried Manchego Cheese

Paté de Hongos   96
Mushroom Paté with Roasted
Garlic and Oloroso

Ñoquis en Salsa de Cabrales   97
Potato Gnocchi in Blue Cheese
Cream with Porcini Mushrooms

Salmorejo   98
Thick Tomato Bread Puree

Pipérade   100
Red Pepper Stew

Piquillos Confitados   101
Piquillo-Garlic Confit with
Shaved Idiazabal

Hummus   103
Garbanzo-Carrot Hummus
with Grilled Yogurt Flatbread

Mozzarella Parrilla   105
Grilled Mozzarella Skewers

Pisto Manchego   106
Vegetable Stew with Fried Egg

Pimientos Rellenos   109
Green Chiles Stuffed with Cheese

Seafood Tapas

Cataplana   112
Clam Stew in a Copper Pot

Gambas Andaluz   115
Fried Shrimp

Bonito Crudo   116
Tuna Carpaccio

Esparrogos con Salmone   119
Asparagus with Smoked
Salmon and Goat Cheese

Pinchos de Boquerone
y Romesco   120
Olive Oil Toasts with Pickled
Anchovies and Romesco Sauce

Pulpo en Vinegretta   123
Octopus in Vinaigrette

Calamares a la Plancha   125
Grilled Squid with Squid Ink
and Piquillo Pepper Puree

Pulpo Frito   126
Crispy Fried Octopus with Salmon
Roe Aioli and Pickled Green Chiles

> continued

Puré de Bacaloa 129
Salt Cod Puree with Egg and Toast

Gambas a la Plancha 131
Flat-Grilled Shrimp with Pimenton
and Shaved Marcona Almonds

Pinchos de Cangrejo 132
Crab Salad Toasts

*Pinchos de Bonito y
Idiazabal* 134
Tuna Toasts with Melted Idiazabal

Boquerones con Queso 135
White Anchovies Stuffed
with Goat Cheese

Langosta Cus Cus 135
Lobster with Saffron Couscous,
Idiazabal, and Piquillos

Tortillitas 137
Shrimp Pancakes

Canelones del Mare 138
Rolled Pasta with Scallop and Crab

Pez Espada 141
Grilled Swordfish with
Pomegranate

Gambas Moros 143
Moroccan Grilled Shrimp

*Croquettas de Cangrejo
y Manchego* 144
Manchego Crab Croquettes

Salmone Curado Oloroso 145
Cured Salmon

Vieras con Morcilla 146
Seared Sea Scallops with Morcilla
and Passion Fruit Cream

Mejillones con Romesco 149
Mussels Steamed in
Romesco Fish Broth

Coca de Boquerones 150
White Anchovy Flatbread
with Roncal Cheese

Vieras con Mahon 151
Sea Scallops with Orange-Parsnip
Puree and Mahon Cheese

Sardinas Asadas 152
Grilled Sardines with Grilled
Lemon Vinaigrette

Meat Tapas

Serranitos 156
Pork, Jamón, and Green
Pepper Toasts

*Pinchos de Chorizo y Huevo
de Codorniz* 158
Chorizo Toasts with
Fried Quail Eggs

Rilletes de Cerdo 159
Chilled Cooked Pork in Pork Fat

Buey con Caramelo 161
Grilled Beef with Smoked
Sea Salt Caramel

Carne Crudo 162
Raw Beef with Preserved Lemons,
Piquillos, and Garlic Aioli

Pinchos de Pollo 164
Grilled Chicken Skewers
with Harissa Couscous

Cantimpalitos 167
Grilled Mini Chorizos
with Potato Puree

Morcilla con Manzanas 168
Blood Sausage with Apples

Patatas al Ajillo con Chorizo 169
Potatoes with Chorizo

Morcilla con Setas 170
Blood Sausage with Mushrooms,
Spring Peas, and Mint Oil

Kefta 173
Grilled Ground Lamb

Canelones de Morcilla 174
Blood Sausage-and-Beet Canelones

Corazon 175
Grilled Beef Heart with Romesco

Pollo con Pedro Ximenez 176
PX Chicken with Garlic
and Oranges

Higado de Pato 177
Foie Gras with PX Glaze
and Grilled Pineapple

Pato con Idiazabal 178
Pan-Seared Duck Breast with
Melted Idiazabal, Mango,
and Smoky Cashew Butter

*Garbanzos con
Chicharrónes* 180
Chickpeas with Lamb
Chicharrónes

Acknowledgments

Thanks to:

Leslie, Emma and Liam, Gibbs Smith, Ilana Blankman, Jose Rodriguez, Sandra and the pastry team, Manuel Luis Suarez, Adam Johnson, Goler Shoes, Doug Merriam, Santa Fe School of Cooking and the entire Curtis Family, Hutton Broadcasting, LuXX Hotel, Inger at the St. Francis, Frankie Lucero, Raul Chico Goler, Miguel Villalpando, Jade Adams, Masa at Sushi Land East, Il Piatto, Matt and Honey, Guadalupe Goler and family, Katelin Walters, Eric Stapelman, Marty and Nancy Spei, Mark and Nicole Tobiessen, Nacha Mendez, Bralt Bralds, Rocky Durham, Ricardo Martinez, Roland Van Loon, the Mudponies, Jono Manson, Loren Nickell-Jones, Susanna Bustamante, Kaitlin Walters, Elena Ailes, Alena Morales, Maria and Lawrence Baca and family, Hugh Elliot, Evoke Gallery, InArt Gallery, Blue Rain Gallery, Rob DeWalt, Johnny V, Larry and Design Warehouse, Paul D. Dominico and family, *Santa Fe Reporter,* Gweneth Dolan, Sam Shepard, Giada DeLaurentis, Ginny Walden, The Spanish Table, Basque Club, Ted Nugent, Lola and Miguel, Beti Jai, La Cuchara de San Telmo, Gerry Dawes, the Sherry Council of America, Copa Jerez, Heidi Stine and TAPAS, Rouge Cat, Action Coach, AWFS, the *New York Times,* Welcome to Bohemia, Jambo Café, Plaza Café, Oliver Ridgeway, Just the Best, Matt Romero, Santa Fe Farmers Market, The Bullring, Greg O'Byrne, Chango (the Band), Maris Hutchinsen, Colleen Hayes, Conrad Crespin, Aaron Crespin, Jill Cashman, Jay Romero, Shar Ximenez, Doug and Sharron Gray, Cynthia and Ian and family, Serena, Gerry Dawes, Mark Miller, David Sellers, Mark Kiffin, Santa Luna, Local Flavor, Fiasco Wines, Classical Wines, Lily and Charlie O'Leary, Cooking with Kids, Santa Fe Wine and Chile Fiesta, Los Gatos, La Anchoita, Miguel and Lola, Santa Fe Community College, Joe Fuka, Jean Moore, Pais Vasco, Euskadi, Kathie DiCorta, and Paul Hunsicker, Miguel Velasquez, Campbells, Sweeneys, Farrows, Foti family, Kenneys, Adelmans, Nardelli family, Leslie V. Campbell.

Nuances of Spanish Flavor

Why do some cultures, some countries, some cities, and some families have great food and others do not? The answer resides in the group's willingness to deem cooking important. When you go anywhere in Spain, you realize in the first ten minutes that cooking is very important to these people. By the end of the day you realize it is not just important, it is sacred. There is a long and well-celebrated culinary history there. The Spaniards have great strength of character, which makes them proud and exuberant cooks. Their complex reality weaves a story of many cultures with sometimes tumultuously opposing political histories. Moors, Basques, Celts, Romans, and French have all contributed to this mosaic. There is intense feeling and emotion toward food that is deeply rooted in the Spanish identity. Life in Spain can be delicate—like saffron and honey—or fierce—like bold peppers and chorizos. History and passion combine to make the cuisine a celebration and extension of this great heritage.

As a chef and a cook, I like to absorb ideas and bits of information from lots of sources that will combine to make me a better cook. I have been a chef and student of Spanish cooking for many years. There is a deep, fertile spring of inspiration to be found here. This book is the result of getting to know the ingredients and trial and error with using different flavor combinations.

So, rather than documenting classic regional dishes, what I offer the reader here is a journal of recipes that are a result of my exploring flavors. The style of these recipes could be classified as a blend of traditional and modern. I do not try to replicate the classics when I cook. Instead I immerse myself in the mind-set of great cooking, which should be a balance of knowing the traditional ingredients, techniques, and flavor combinations without letting these limit the imagination.

I discuss specific ingredients, flavors, and recipes in the pages that follow. But there are layers of flavors and hidden nuances that are not found in the recipes themselves. There is much to learn from this vast culinary landscape that can make us better cooks. I do not talk about having expensive knives and copper cookware, the latest food processor or watching the chefs on the food channel. None of these things will improve your cooking. Simply ask yourself when you are enjoying a great meal, "Why does this taste so good?" Here are a few answers my focus on Spanish cooking has revealed.

National pride is a flavor

The bustling streets of Madrid are alive with exuberance and pride. The cuisine is an integral part of life. The tapas bars are a proud display of jamón, chorizo, manchego, and olive oil. Madrilenos have a robust appetite for the real thing and enjoy educating visitors on their authentic dishes. Chefs at the food markets have strong relationships with growers, suppliers, and vendors. These relationships are vital and many were formed over generations. Again, cooking is important! Very basic, down-to-earth flavors can yield thrilling and sophisticated results when these relationships remain intact. Cooking is done with pride and is worn like a badge of honor.

Tradition adds flavor

A great culture is one that is well defined. To know the traditions and to love them and hold them sacred gives tremendous strength and foundation, and only then can you face the rest of the world with fearlessness. The biggest fear for someone holding to traditional culture in the modern age is that they will go too far, be left out on a limb, become lost and unable to find their way back. When the tradition is strong, there is no doubt that it will stay intact no matter how far you go.

Spaniards were able to literally go out to all corners of the earth exploring and conquering new worlds. They leapt fearlessly into the unknown. My favorite example of this is in the city of San Sebastian, where the old-world food traditions are solidly ingrained and deliciously evident when you stroll down the street. It does not surprise me, then, given my theory explained above, that this was also the birthplace of the greatest innovations in modern gastronomy and continues to redefine where the cutting edge is. In fact, this pattern is well documented in many areas of Basque life.

Exuberance adds flavor

"Keep the capacity to be surprised," as famous Basque chef Juan Mari Arzak says. Passionate cooks cannot hide their affection for a perfectly ripe tomato or deny that the aroma of fresh bread can be the source of an emotional experience. New dishes will inspire more cooking, and the excitement builds in anticipation of what is yet to come in the culinary world. This is unfinished business and the surprises will keep flowing.

History adds flavor

The walls of the Parte Vieja, the cultural center and Old Town of San Sebastian, have a patina created by generations of aromas, day after day after day. Layers of flavor and commitment can be tasted in the small bakeries and *pinchos* bars every day. Also, the older folks are out and about in the bars and cafes and not at home in a rocking chair. They seem as if they are keeping a watchful eye on the food and making sure it is right.

Respect adds flavor

Every good cook has great affection and respect for the ingredients. The best cooks are open to being inspired and guided by the ingredients and are not trying to control and manipulate them.

A tablespoon of everyday life

Everything you do in the kitchen—even your thoughts, emotions, and presence of mind—will affect the flavor of your cooking. The way you think about ingredients, the way you move in the kitchen, the people you cook with, and the feeling you have toward the occasion you are cooking for all impact the flavor of your dishes. Genuinely wanting to please the recipients of your cooking is one of the best flavors! Cooking is tightly connected to the most intimate and essential aspects of life: family, tradition, health, happiness, celebration, social life, and etc. Our life and culture tells us when to cook, how to cook, when to eat, and with whom we should cook and eat. Our relationship to ingredients also enhances our relationship to the natural world and our environment.

The love you have for the ocean and the fish in it adds flavor

On a recent trip to Sanlucar de Barremeda, a fishing village in Andalucia in the sherry triangle, where fish is caught and consumed in quantities that defy mathematics, a fisherman said to me, "The ocean must love us because it gives us a daily feast. Like mother's milk."

"Proverbs are short sentences drawn from long and wise experience," wrote Miguel Cervantes in *Don Quixote* (1605). The same can be said of recipes: they are short statements that rely on generations of trial and error and experience. Most times when a chef comes up with something new, it is based on a traditional flavor combination that was established long before he was born. The cooking tradition continues and we can all participate in it. This book shares my thoughts about food and cooking and continues this legacy. I will always be inspired by artisanal ingredients, energized by cooks and chefs I have met along the way, and forever committed to cooking a memorable meal. *Buen provecho!*

Spanish Ingredients

Having access to artisanal ingredients inspires great cooking. Such ingredients are brought to the table with passion, superior skill level, and respect for tradition. Many of these items are regulated and classified with Denomination of Origin status. This is an official designation for food products that are differentiated by such features as their geographical origin, the method of preparation, and the source of the raw materials used.

Spain is a large country with diverse climates, tastes, and cultural influences. There has always been an energetic compulsion to reap the glorious bounty of the land, which is impressive. Spain is the largest producer of wine, olives, and olive oil in the world. It also produces more cheese than any other nation and consumes a huge amount of seafood, second only to Japan. So respect for the ingredients is not only built into the culture, but many of the laws of the DO are protected and enforced by the Spanish Government and EU laws.

Here is a short list of some of the ingredients that are available in the United States and offer endless inspiration chefs and home cooks to live with more enjoyment!

Spanish Cheeses

Rich grazing lands provide Spain with great numbers of cows, sheep and goats. An impressive variety of cheeses are produced in respect to traditional methods and a watchful DO commission.

For hundreds of years Spain has achieved a consistent level of high quality cheeses in a great variety of textures and depth of flavors. Cow, sheep and goat milks are well represented along with a number of mixed milk cheeses here are a few of the most popular:

Manchego—The famous semi-hard sheep's milk cheese from La Mancha is available aged for five months or one year. Most often served in tapas bars swimming in extra virgin olive oil, it is simply, one of the best products Spain has to offer.

Idiazabal—Firm, nutty, and buttery, this slightly smoky Laxta sheep's milk cheese from the Basque country is a well-loved staple of this magical region. On a recent trip to San Sebastian, a Basque cook stopped me in my tracks with fried croquettas oozing with Idiazabal.

Mahon—This very versatile cow's milk cheese is from Menorca. It is sweet, creamy and slightly salty (the grazing grasses on the island of Menorca have a high sea salt content.) This cheese is often enjoyed on its own, but it is superb melted in hot dishes like pasta or rice or sea scallops.

Roncal—This semi-hard sheep's milk cheese has been made the same way for about 3,000 years. Sheep are grazed in the rich Roncal Valley in Navarro. The flavor is tangy, with herbal and grassy aromas. It shreds nicely over soups and salads. This is the perfect cheese to eat simply sliced while you uncork a bottle of Tempranillo and contemplate the meaning of 3,000 years of cheese-making.

Tetilla—A creamy cow's milk cheese made in the Galicia, tetilla it is extremely popular all over Spain and is gaining notoriety in the States. It gets its name from its unique shape, with a small nipple, or *tetilla*, at the top. Children love the mild flavor. It is often served with fruit as a dessert but melts well in chile peppers.

Cabrales—This strong blue cheese disturbs and awakens parts of the psyche that would otherwise remain oblivious to the outside world. We are thrill seekers, risk takers, sensationalists; we suspect something that triggers such alarm could have a sweet reward. In this case, we are right. The pungent and rich blue cheese from the Asturias region is often made with mixed milk of cow, sheep, and goat, depending on availability and season. Try it crumbled on steak, melted into pasta, or drizzled with honey for a surprising dessert.

Torta del Casar—My friend and Spanish food and wine guru Gerry Dawes lovingly describes one of the best cheeses in the world:

"A raw sheep's milk cheese from villages near the provincial capital of Cáceres in the Extremadura region of west central Spain. Rustic, delicious, creamy, buttery, hints of dill and thyme, with an assertive, but pleasant finish. Very rich, fairly intense and flavorful cheese that is delightfully creamy and spreadable in the springtime versions. Very similar in style to the French vacherin Mont d'Or, except that it is not made with cows' milk. Torta del Casar and its cousin cheese, Torta de la Serena, use only wild milk thistle rennet to coagulate the milk, which is an ancient Moorish and Jewish dietary custom."

Cured Meats: Morcilla, Chorizo, Jamón Serrano

Quality, tradition, and pride are the common adjectives for these products. Chorizos are sausages in different shapes and flavors. Some varieties are fresh, but most are cured and slightly smoked and can be eaten without cooking. A typical tapa is sliced chorizo with bread and olives or cheese. Morcilla is a special type of chorizo more like a blood pudding made from pork blood, pork meat, and pork fat. Jamón serrano is probably the most famous product in all of Spain: the cured hind quarters of pigs.

Chorizo pimenton—Usually firm, dry, fully cured, and lightly smoked and spiced with pimenton, smoked paprika. Great for slicing and eating with cheese.

Chistorra—a longer and thinner chorizo popular in the Basque region, it has hearty, intense flavor without being spicy.

Cantimpalitos—small chorizos, semi-cured. Great on the grill or cooked with eggs.

Buttifaria—Catalonian white sausage made with a puree of the best pork and garlic. This fresh sausage is great on the grill or cooked with beans.

Sobrasada—a soft spreadable sausage that makes a terrific tapa on bread and served hot out of the oven. Sometimes this is served with a drizzle of honey.

Salchichon—a spicy, dry, cured sausage similar to Italian salami. Chunks of fat are folded into the mix for a nice marbling effect. Serve sliced thinly on bread.

Morcilla—a pork blood sausage that is available in both fresh and cured versions. These tasty black sausages are a great ingredient for soups and stews and pair well with lots of other ingredients. This represents an ancient traditional method of using every part of the pig.

Jamón serrano—These hams are cured in the unique climate of mountain drying rooms for almost two years following an ancient process from before Roman times. This a specialty item is served all over the world.

Jamón Iberico—The cured hind leg of the semi-wild Pata Negra pigs, which feed on acorns, give this ham a rich, nutty, exquisite flavor. Nothing else is needed with this ham. Enjoy the rich smoky saltiness as the thin slices melt on your tongue. Due to the pigs' acorn diet, the fats in jamón Iberico are very high in oleic acid, which is a proven benefit to cholesterol level.

Olives

Probably *the* defining flavor of Spanish cuisine, olives have been grown since ancient times in diverse varieties of color, flavor, and aroma. Spain is the leading producer of olives in the world, and these little morsels have been of huge significance to the economy, health, cuisine, and philosophy of this great nation. Here are just a few varieties:

Arbequina—a tasty small, almost round, brownish snacking olive that also makes a delicately flavored olive oil.

Manzanilla—a medium-size green olive with a slightly nutty and smoky flavor.

Empeltre—a deep, dark purple olive with a sweet-tart flavor that goes well with sherry and salty seafood.

Aragon—a rich, meaty black olive, fleshy and soft and overripe. This one is great for olive paste and purees.

Olive Oil

Spain's warm sunny climate gives birth to more extra virgin olive oil than any other country. It is known for its superior quality and is sold around the globe. It is obviously a key element to the cuisine and is found in almost every recipe—even in many desserts. The International Olive Council (IOC) is an intergovernmental organization based in Madrid, with 23 member states. The IOC promotes olive oil around the world by tracking production, defining quality standards, and monitoring authenticity.

Olive oils, especially from the Andalucian region, are loaded with antioxidants and have many proven health benefits. These oils are used for all types of cooking. In Southern Spain, where the cooks are masterful at the art of fried fish, they fry in nothing but extra virgin olive oil. The oil will not burn and adds great flavor to the end product.

Sherry Vinegar

To be called *vinagre de Jerez,* by law the sherry vinegar must be aged at least 6 months in American oak barrels, it must be produced in the Sherry Triangle DO region near the towns of Jerez de La Frontera, Sanlucar de Barrameda, and El Puerto de Santa Maria. Most sherry vinegars are aged in the same solera process that is used for aging sherry.

Peppers

Probably the most important vegetable in Spanish cooking, peppers, or chiles, came from the New World when Columbus sent them to the monasteries of Spain in 1493.

Green and red bell peppers are used in great adundance in a wide variety of dishes. Here are a few other chiles or pimientos (peppers):

Pimiento de Gernika—a medium-sized Basque green pepper, mild in flavor and often served fried in olive oil with seafood or its own.

Pimiento de pardon—a small, delicate green chile from the Galicia region. A popular bar snack, it is fried in olive oil with sea salt and garlic. As the Spanish say, "Somos picon, otros, non": Some are hot, some are not.

Piquillo—a sweet and slightly smoky red pepper. Piquillos are eaten all over Spain and are often found in jars already roasted and peeled. When the firm flesh is in one piece, these are perfect for stuffing.

Piparra—a fresh, small, slender green pepper from Northern Spain. It is most commonly found pickled in vinegar and adds a spicy, piquant flavor balance to rich foods. When piparras ripen to red, they are strung up and dried in the sun and are called guindillas. These are crushed into dishes when a little hot spice is in order.

Nora—a dried round red pepper that has deep flavors of the tobacco and bitter dried fruit. Often found in ground powder form.

Pimenton

Handmade smoked paprika is a versatile spice in Spanish cooking. It adds a unique robust and rustic flavor to soups, stews, grilled seafood, and rice dishes. Several varieties of small red peppers are smoke-dried in large drying houses for about two weeks. The chiles are exposed to large amounts of oak smoke to give it a distinctive concentrated smoky flavor.

Pimenton Dulce—made with round, sweet peppers for a mild paprika.

Pimenton Agridulce—made with dried peppers with medium heat.

Pimenton Picante—made with a mixture of elongated hot chiles and can be very spicy and smoky.

There are also many varieties of non-smoked paprika that are very good and that come in a variety of heat levels.

Marcona Almonds

Marcona almonds are rounder, softer, and more delicate than California almonds. Marconas have a rich, sweet flavor and are included in many recipes here and throughout Spain. They are quite often found lightly fried in olive oil and sprinkled with sea salt. We like to toss in some pimenton for a tasty tapa.

Blood Oranges and Pomegranates

Brought to Spain by the Moors, these fruits add a healthy dose of energy to dishes with their vibrant flavors and electric colors. These are found in salads, seafood, and savory dishes as well as sweet.

Some of my favorite uses:

- Grilled sardine salad with frisee, fennel, and pomegranate seeds
- Swordfish grilled with pomegranate
- Blood orange aioli for raw fish
- Blood orange sangria
- Tarta morada, a blood orange and pomegranate tart

Boquerones and Anchoas

Filleted white anchovies are preserved in vinegar, garlic, and a small amount of olive oil. The vinegar bleaches the flesh of these little fish and gives them a bright, refreshing quality that surprises people who have a preconceived idea about how an anchovy should taste.

Some of my favorite uses:

- On a plate with some shavings of orange zest and a drizzle of olive oil.
- Stuffed with goat cheese
- On top of ensaladilla rusa (the ubiquitous Spanish potato salad with conserved tuna)
- Anchoas are large anchovies that are packed in olive oil and sea salt and have deeper, meatier flavor than the boquerones.
- Simply out of the can on top of bread toasted in olive oil, a favorite in the tapas bars.
- With fig and goat cheese

Conservas

Spaniards have a passion and skill with expertly preserved fish in cans. These products capture and preserve the sweet meats of the sea. The cans are bursting with fresh saltwater ocean flavors when opened a year later. The wide variety includes sardines, mackerel, clams, mussels, razor clams, tuna, and anchovies. When you order these at a tapas bar, many times the bartender will pull the top back and serve it to you still in the can, with some bread or potato chips.

Saffron

Brought to Spain by the Moors along with oranges, almonds, and honey, saffron is the stamen of the crocus. It has been cultivated for over 4,000 years and has many uses in traditional and modern medicine. Cooks prize the flavor and aroma of saffron because of its unique and pungent perfume and sweet aroma of honey and fresh grass. The color it adds to foods like paella and saffron fish broth is vibrant and appetizing. It remains the most expensive spice because it must be harvested by hand and takes a great deal of space to grow. A football field of crocus is needed to produce one pound of saffron, which will be worth about $3,000 on the American market.

Fresh Fish

Spain consumes more seafood per person than any other country except Japan. The variety pulled from the waters surrounding the peninsula is put to good use. Famous dishes include bacaloa (salt cod), trout, calamari, tunas, octopus, langostinos, mussels, clams, oysters, and *gambas al ajillo*.

The daily catch is taken into the town markets and sells out in a few hours. "The ocean must love us to give us such a feast every day," say the fishermen in the village of Sanlucar de Barrameda, Southern Spain.

Bacalao (Salt Cod)

Cod fish that has been salted, dried, and preserved is later de-salted and hydrated to make some of the most loved dishes in Spain. Bacalao is eaten in huge quantities in Spain. The process of drying and rehydrating gives the fish a unique flavor and texture.

Spanish Wines

Any discussion of Spanish food is incomplete without talking about wine. All of the history, skill, and passion that go into the ingredients and cooking in Spain are equaled in wine production. From sophisticated and world-renowned wines to basic table wine and chatos served in little glasses at the tapas bars, the food and wine are inseparable. Spain's landscape is almost covered with grapes. Almost 18 percent of the world's vineyards are in Spain. This huge number means that a great portion of the country is dedicated to wine. Spain has 65 DO wine regions.

Sherry (or Vinos de Jerez or simply, Jerez)

The ancient art of sherry making continues in the unique micro climate of the sherry triangle in Southern Spain. The towns of Jerez de la Frontera, San Lucar de Barremeda, and Puerto de Santa Maria have perfect natural conditions for growing the Palomino grapes and aging the fortified wines in a complex solera system that gives sherry its characteristic blend of vintages.

Sherry pairs perfectly with food. The sherries range in style from salty, dry finos to fragrant, nutty amontillados, rich and lavish olorosos, and syrupy sweet Pedro Ximenez.

Add some Spanish ingredients to your pantry and enjoy the distinct, delicious flavors of Spain when you make the recipes that follow.

Salads

Bonito con Pimientos Verdes

Tuna with Fried Green Peppers, Olives, and Tomatoes

A simply exquisite version of the beloved combo of tuna and olives.

Serves 6

6 (3-ounce) tuna steaks

Sea salt and black pepper to taste

1 cup olive oil, divided

2 Anaheim or New Mexico green chiles

1 poblano chile

4 cloves garlic, slivered

2 tablespoons sherry vinegar

1 cup pitted black olives

2 cups cherry tomatoes, halved

Season the tuna steaks with salt and pepper. Heat a skillet with ¼ cup olive oil on high heat, and cook the tuna for about 4 minutes per side, until cooked through. Remove tuna from pan and set aside to cool.

In the same pan, add the remaining olive oil and turn the heat on high. Cut all the chiles into strips and fry for about 5 minutes, until browned and soft. Add the garlic and cook for another 3 minutes, until soft and cooked through. Remove pan from the heat and whisk in the sherry vinegar. Set aside to cool to room temperature.

Slice each tuna steak into ¼-inch strips. Toss all ingredients from the sauté pan into a bowl with the olives and tomatoes. Gently toss the tuna strips into the bowl, and divide the mixture onto six small plates.

Ensalada Parrilla

Grilled Tomatoes and Romaine with Sherry Vinaigrette and Shaved Manchego

This salad is perfect with a simple grilled steak.

Serves 6

12 crispy romaine leaves

1/2 cup extra virgin olive oil, divided

Salt and pepper to taste

24 (1/2-inch) slices ripe tomato

3 tablespoons sherry vinegar

4-ounce wedge of manchego cheese

Heat a grill to medium-high. Toss the romaine leaves in a bowl with 1/4 cup olive oil, salt, and pepper. Grill for 2 minutes, turning the leaves with tongs. Remove and set aside.

Toss the tomatoes with 2 tablespoons olive oil and some salt and pepper. Grill for about 2 minutes per side, until tomatoes are lightly charred.

Toss the tomatoes and romaine leaves in a bowl with the rest of the olive oil and vinegar. Divide the mixture onto six small plates, giving each serving roughly the same amount of lettuce and tomato. Spoon the remaining dressing from the bowl onto the salads. With a vegetable peeler, cut a few shavings of manchego on top of each serving.

Ensalada de Piquillo y Queso de Cabra

Goat Cheese and Piquillo Pepper Salad with Romaine Leaves and Grilled Fig-Mustard Vinaigrette

Contrasting tastes and textures abound in this salad: soft, creamy goat cheese, crisp romaine crunch, sweet/smoky peppers, and tangy pickled onions.

Serves 8

1 pound fresh goat cheese

1 jar (12 ounces) Spanish piquillo
   peppers, drained, julienned

Grilled Fig-Mustard Vinaigrette
   (see facing page)

16 crisp romaine leaves

Cracked black pepper

Pickled Red Onion (see facing page)

Form goat cheese into 16 (1-ounce) balls. In a large bowl, toss cheese and peppers with ½ cup of the Grilled Fig-Mustard Vinaigrette. Arrange 2 romaine leaves on each plate. Top with cheese-pepper mixture, 2 cheese balls per plate. Drizzle some of the remaining vinaigrette on the plates, being sure to dress the romaine. Finish plates with cracked black pepper and some Pickled Red Onion.

Grilled Fig-Mustard Vinaigrette

Makes about 2 cups

8 fresh figs, cut in half*

2 tablespoons plus 1 1/2 cups olive oil, divided

Salt and pepper to taste

1 tablespoon whole grain Dijon mustard

2 teaspoons honey

1 teaspoon aged sherry vinegar

Heat a gas or charcoal grill to medium heat. In a medium-size bowl, toss figs with 2 tablespoons olive oil; sprinkle with salt and pepper. Grill 2 minutes per side, until figs are heated. Put grilled figs in a food processor with mustard, honey and vinegar. Process until pureed. With the motor running, slowly add 1 1/2 cups olive oil. Season to taste.

If fresh figs are not available, pour 1/4 cup boiling water over 10 chopped dried figs; let stand until cooled. Continue with recipe, using figs and water.

Pickled Red Onion

1 cup boiling water

1 medium red onion, halved lengthwise,
  thinly sliced lengthwise

1/4 cup fresh orange juice

1/4 cup fresh lime juice

2 tablespoons white wine vinegar

1 teaspoon dried Mexican
  oregano leaves, crumbled

1 teaspoon sugar

1/2 teaspoon salt

2 whole cloves

Pour boiling water over onion in a small bowl. Let stand until softened, about 10 minutes. Drain onion well and return to bowl. Stir in all remaining ingredients. Set aside.

Ensalada de Gambas

Shrimp and Fennel Salad with Grapefruit Aioli

The shrimp are pan-seared and then tossed with the salad so that you experience hot, cold, and the crunch of fresh fennel.

Serves 6

1 egg

2 whole cloves garlic

1 tablespoon lemon juice

1 cup olive oil, divided

2 grapefruits, sectioned; divided

12 large shrimp, peeled and deveined

Salt and pepper to taste

2 tablespoons chopped parsley

2 cloves garlic, slivered

3 fennel bulbs, cleaned and
  cored, thinly julienned

1 red onion, julienned

To make an aioli, put the egg, garlic, and lemon juice into a blender. Puree well. While the motor is still running, slowly pour in $3/4$ cup olive oil. Then add 6 sections of grapefruit and a pinch of salt. Set aside.

Season the shrimp with salt, pepper, and parsley. Heat a sauté pan with the remaining oil. Cook the shrimp along with the slivered garlic on high heat for about 2 minutes per side, until the shrimp turn pink. In a bowl, toss the shrimp, fennel, onion, and remaining grapefruit sections with 4 tablespoons of aioli. Divide onto six small plates, giving each plate 2 shrimp. Spoon a tablespoon of aioli onto each plate.

Lechuga Romana con Cabrales

Romaine Salad with Blue Cheese and Roasted Apple–Piñon Dressing

I like to celebrate the fall season with this salad, when the apples are the best.

Serves 8

Roasted Apple–Piñon Dressing

4 Granny Smith apples, peeled,
  cored and cut in half

$1/2$ cup olive oil, divided

3 tablespoons apple cider vinegar, divided

Salt and pepper to taste

2 tablespoons honey

$1^1/2$ cups toasted pine nuts, divided

Salad

5 cups chopped romaine

1 cup crumbled blue cheese

Preheat oven to 350 degrees.

Toss apples with a few tablespoons of olive oil, a splash of vinegar and salt and pepper. Roast in a baking dish in the oven for 30 minutes. Transfer apples and all drippings to a food processor along with the remaining vinegar, honey, and 1 cup pine nuts. Puree well. While the motor is running, add remaining olive oil. Taste and adjust salt and pepper.

Toss the dressing with the romaine. Arrange on plates and top each salad with crumbled blue cheese and the remaining toasted pine nuts.

Ensalada de Naranjas y Boquerones

Salad with Oranges, Fennel, Anchovies, and Manzanilla Vinaigrette

This is perfect summertime eating, with the flavors of the southern sherry region.

Serves 6

2 fennel bulbs, cored and julienned very thin

2 oranges, sectioned

4 ounces pickled white anchovies

Manzanilla Vinaigrette

¼ cup extra virgin olive oil

¼ cup orange juice

½ cup Manzanilla olives

3 tablespoons Manzanilla sherry

Salt and pepper to taste

Toss all ingredients well in a bowl. Divide onto 6 small plates
and serve at room temperature.

Ensalada de Piquillo Parrilla

Grilled Piquillo with Chopped Eggs, White Anchovies, and Olive Oil

These ingredients can be used in almost endless combinations because they are always good together.

Serves 6

12 canned or jarred piquillo peppers

1/4 cup olive oil, divided

Salt, divided

6 hard boiled eggs

12 white anchovies

1/4 cup chopped fresh parsley

Heat a grill to medium-high heat. Toss the piquillos with a few tablespoons of olive oil and a teaspoon of salt, and grill for about 2 minutes per side to heat through. Transfer to a large plate. Cut the eggs in quarters and arrange on top of the peppers. Lay the anchovies on top. Sprinkle with salt, parsley, and remaining olive oil.

Tomates Andaluz

Marinated Tomatoes with Mint Vinaigrette Andalusian Style with Sherry Vinegar, Cumin, and Garlic

This Andalusian-style salad is perfect to share among friends, with some grilled sardines and crusty bread.

Serves 6

4 ripe tomatoes, sliced

Mint Vinaigrette Andalusian Style

2 cloves garlic, minced

2 tablespoons chopped mint

3 tablespoons sherry vinegar

¼ cup extra virgin olive oil

2 teaspoons salt

1 tablespoon toasted cumin seed

Lay the tomatoes on a large plate. Mix the dressing by whisking together remaining ingredients. Pour the mixture over the tomatoes and let marinate for 1 hour at room temperature. Serve with crusty bread.

Ensalada Mediterranean

Mediterranean Salad with Figs, Apricots, Feta, and Olives

This dish shows off some ancient Mediterranean ingredients and flavor combinations.

Serves 8

1 cup white wine

1/2 cup dried apricots

1/2 cup dried black figs

3 tablespoons sherry vinegar

3/4 cup extra virgin olive oil

1/4 cup honey

1 tablespoon salt

2 teaspoons cracked black pepper

4 cups mixed baby greens

1 cup pitted black olives

4 ounces sheep feta cheese, crumbled

Heat the wine in a small saucepan and add the apricots and dried figs.
Cook on low heat for about 5 minutes; set aside to cool. Whisk together
the vinegar, oil, honey, salt, and pepper. In a bowl, toss the greens with
the dressing, dried fruits, olives, and feta. Mix well. Divide onto small
plates for a salad course.

Manchego en Salsa de Tomate

Marinated Manchego in Fresh Tomato, Olive Oil, and Sherry Vinegar

A simple starter of cubed Manchego cheese could make a spectacular kick-off to a dinner party.

Serves 6

1 pound manchego cheese

3 ripe tomatoes

1/2 cup Spanish olive oil

1 tablespoon sherry vinegar

Pinch of salt

Cut the cheese into 1-inch cubes and place in a bowl. Cut the tomatoes in half and grate them with a cheese grater over the bowl of cheese. Stir in the oil, vinegar, and salt. Let this marinate at room temperature for 1 hour. Divide among small glass bowls. Serve with toothpicks.

Arugula con Cabrales y Granada

Cabrales Pomegranate Salad with Arugula

Crushed walnuts can be added for an extra layer of texture.

Serves 6

1/4 cup extra virgin olive oil

2 tablespoons sherry vinegar

2 tablespoons pomegranate molasses

1 teaspoon salt

2 teaspoons cracked black pepper

4 cups fresh arugula

4 ounces crumbled Cabrales blue cheese

1/2 cup pomegranate seeds

Make a dressing by whisking together the oil, vinegar, molasses, salt, and pepper. In a bowl, toss the arugula with the dressing and cheese. Divide onto small plates. Add pomegranate seeds and garnish the plate with a few grindings of black pepper.

Manchego en Salsa de Tomate

Ensalada de Jamón y Alcachofas

Arugula with Jamón, Grilled Artichokes, and Aged Sherry Vinegar Reduction

A flashy modern-style presentation of old-world flavors.

Serves 6

2 cups aged sherry vinegar

6 medium-size artichokes

4 cups fresh arugula

¼ cup extra virgin olive oil

1 teaspoon salt

2 teaspoons cracked black pepper

6 slices jamón serrano

1 cup Pickled Red Onion (see page 33)

In a small saucepan over high heat, cook the sherry vinegar until it reduces to about ¼ cup. Set aside to cool. Grill the artichokes as explained on page 77.

Toss the arugula with olive oil, salt, and pepper. Prepare six chilled salad plates. Lay a slice of jamón serrano on each plate. Divide dressed arugula among the plates on top of the jamón. Divide Pickled Red Onion on top of each bed of arugula and place a grilled artichoke on top. Drizzle all plates with a teaspoon of reduced sherry vinegar.

Soups and Stews

Sopa de Cebolla

Sweet Onion Soup with Amontillado and Cabrales

A bit like the neighboring French onion soup with a blast of the noble Cabrales blue cheese.

Serves 6

6 medium yellow onions, julienned

¼ cup extra virgin olive oil

2 tablespoons butter

2 tablespoons sherry vinegar

1 tablespoon salt

2 teaspoons black pepper

4 cups beef stock

1 tablespoon fresh thyme leaves

2 cups amontillado sherry

6 ounces Cabrales blue cheese, crumbled

In a soup pot, sauté the onions at medium-low heat with olive oil, butter, vinegar, salt, and pepper until caramelized. Keep cooking for 1 hour, until onions are very soft and very sweet. Add remaining ingredients except the blue cheese. Bring to a boil. Turn down and let simmer on low heat for 45 minutes. Serve in bowls and top with cheese.

Caracoles

Snails in Saffron-Anise Fish Broth

You can find big kettles of this soup at the Mercado de San Miguel in Madrid. Heady aromas of garlic and licorice will transport you to the fresh fish markets of Spain.

Serves 6

1 yellow onion, diced

12 cloves garlic, minced

6 tablespoons butter

4 tablespoons olive oil

4 ounces anise-flavored liqueur

Pinch of saffron

3 pounds escargot

1 cup chopped parsley

6 cups fish stock

2 teaspoons salt

In a soup pot, sauté the onion and garlic in butter and olive oil on medium heat for 10 minutes. Add the liqueur and saffron; stir well for 1 minute. Add remaining ingredients and cook covered on medium heat for 20 minutes. Serve in bowls with spoons for the broth and small seafood forks or picks to remove the snail meat.

Sopa de Chorizo y Almejas
Chorizo Clam Soup

A nice "made to order" soup that can be cooked minutes before eating. Simple, but relies on good ingredients like Spanish chorizo, fresh clams, and amontillado sherry.

Serves 6

Pinch of saffron

4 tablespoons butter, divided

$1/2$ cup chopped fennel bulb, fronds reserved

$1/2$ medium onion, chopped

$1/4$ cup chopped carrot

$1/4$ cup chopped tomato

36 clams

1 cup chopped good Spanish chorizo

1 cup Spanish sherry, amontillado

1 cup heavy cream

3 tablespoons chopped fresh parsley

4 cups clam juice or fish stock

1 tablespoon chopped fennel fronds

Place the saffron threads in a small saucepan over medium heat and toast them briefly. Add 1 tablespoon butter, fennel bulb, onion, carrot, and tomato. Sauté for about 7 minutes. Add remaining ingredients except the fennel fronds. Cook covered for about 3–4 minutes, until clams pop open. Discard any clams that don't open. Ladle into 6 bowls and garnish with fennel fronds.

Cangrejo Harissa

Crab in Harissa Broth with Couscous

Spicy harissa gives this simple soup an exotic Arabic kick.

Serves 6

Harissa

1 tablespoon coriander seed

1 tablespoon caraway seed

1 teaspoon cumin seed

4 large cloves garlic, unpeeled

4 large red bell peppers

1/2 cup extra virgin olive oil

1 tablespoon sugar

2 tablespoons crushed
   New Mexico red chiles

Salt and pepper to taste

4 cups fish stock

1 cup couscous

1 pound cooked crabmeat

For the harissa: Stir coriander, caraway and cumin in a small skillet over medium-high heat until aromatic, about 30 seconds. Transfer to a food processor. Cook garlic in the same skillet, covered, over medium-low heat until tender, about 10 minutes, turning occasionally. Let garlic cool, then peel it an add to processor. Char bell peppers over a gas flame or in a broiler until blackened on all sides. Enclose in a paper bag; let stand 10 minutes. Peel, seed, and coarsely chop peppers. Add peppers, oil, sugar, and crushed red pepper to processor. Puree. Season with salt and pepper. (Can be made 1 day ahead. Cover and refrigerate.)

Heat the fish stock in a medium-size soup pot. Bring to a boil. Turn down to low and stir in the harissa. Remove from heat and stir in the couscous and crab. Cover and let stand off the heat for 5 minutes. Remove cover, stir, and serve.

Caldo Fino

Beef and Onion Stew with Fino Sherry

The dry fino sherry adds sophistication to this peasant-style stew.

Serves 6

2 pounds cubed stew meat

$1/4$ cup olive oil

2 yellow onions, diced

4 cloves garlic, slivered

2 carrots, diced

1 green pepper, diced

1 pound pearl onions, peeled

4 cups beef stock

4 tomatoes, diced

2 small potatoes, diced

2 bay leaves

2 tablespoons chopped sage

2 guindilla chiles

$1/2$ cup pitted green olives

Salt and black pepper

2 cups fino sherry, divided

In a medium-size soup pot, brown the beef in the oil on medium-high heat. Remove beef and set aside. Add the chopped onions, garlic, carrots, bell pepper, and pearl onions. Cook until soft, about 15 minutes. Add the beef back into the pot. Add remaining ingredients, reserving $1/2$ cup sherry to drizzle on the finished stew. Boil on high heat for 3 minutes, then turn down to low and simmer covered for 3 hours. Serve in bowls and drizzle each bowl with a teaspoon of fino sherry.

Sopa de Higos

Dried Fig and Red Wine Soup with Idiazabal

A classic dried fruit and cheese combination in a new way. The Idiazabal is the distinct, slightly smoky sheep's milk cheese from the Basque region.

Serves 6

2 yellow onions, chopped

4 carrots, chopped

2 cloves garlic, slivered

1/4 cup olive oil

3/4 cup flour

2 cups dried black figs

2 tablespoons sherry vinegar

2 tablespoons honey

1 teaspoon ground clove

1 teaspoon cinnamon

4 cups water

2 cups red wine

Salt and black pepper

4-ounce piece of Idiazabal cheese

In a medium soup pot, sauté the onions, carrots, and garlic in the olive oil over medium-high heat for about 10 minutes. Add the flour and stir. Add remaining ingredients except the cheese and cook over medium heat for 10–15 minutes, until the figs soften. Puree the soup well and serve in bowls. Shave the cheese with a vegetable peeler and place about 1/2 ounce into each bowl of soup.

Caldereta

Shellfish Stew

A simple shellfish stew made rich and velvety with an almond-garlic puree to thicken it. Serve with a glass of amontillado sherry.

Serves 6

Thickener (prepare first and set aside)

1/2 cup extra virgin olive oil

4 large cloves garlic

2 thick slices of baguette

1 cup toasted almonds

1/2 cup chopped parsley

Heat oil in a skillet and fry whole garlic cloves until deep brown in color, about 5–6 minutes. Remove garlic from the pan and set aside. Place the bread in the hot oil and toast on both sides. Combine the bread, garlic, almonds, and parsley in a food processor or use a mortar and pestle. Crush and set aside. This will be used to thicken the stew before serving.

1/2 cup Spanish olive oil

1 yellow onion, finely chopped

1 red bell pepper, cored, seeded, and chopped

2 ounces prosciutto or jamón serrano cut into strips

3 ripe tomatoes, chopped (or use canned tomatoes)

Pinch of saffron threads

1 cup amontillado sherry

2 1/2 cups fish stock

12 clams

12 mussels

6 shrimp, peeled and deveined

1 pound cod

Salt and pepper

Heat the olive oil and sauté onions, peppers, ham, and tomatoes. Cook over medium heat, stirring frequently, for about 15 minutes. Add the saffron and sherry and bring to a boil for 2 minutes. Add the fish stock and bring to a boil. Turn down to medium and add all the seafood. Cover and cook for about 3 minutes, or until clams and mussels open; discard any that fail to open. Stir in the thickener and taste to adjust seasoning.

Sopa de Ajo

Garlic Soup with Bread and Fried Eggs

Very rustic and supremely satisfying.

Serves 6

1 yellow onion, diced

12 cloves garlic, minced

¼ cup extra virgin olive oil

1 cup Sofrito (see page 74)

2 teaspoons salt

2 teaspoons pimenton

12 slices of baguette cut into ½-inch cubes

4 cups chicken stock

6 eggs

In a soup pot, sauté the onion and garlic in olive oil for about 5 minutes on medium heat. Add the sofrito, salt, and pimenton and cook for another 3 minutes. Add the bread and chicken stock and simmer for 15 minutes. Bring to a boil right before serving. Crack a raw egg into each bowl and ladle 6 ounces of hot soup over each egg. The egg will cook but stay slightly runny.

Caldo Pescado Moro

Moorish Fish Soup with Limes, Green Chiles, and Shrimp

Spicy and perfumey Moroccan aromas enhance the briny ocean flavors.

Serves 6

Soup

1 white onion, diced

1/4 cup olive oil

1 green chile, roasted and peeled

2 whole limes, quartered

1 tablespoon minced gingerroot

1 quart fish stock

1/2 pound white fish, cod or halibut

1/2 cup almonds

4 (1-inch-thick) slices baguette, dry

1 bunch cilantro, chopped

3 cloves garlic

1 teaspoon cumin

1/2 teaspoon turmeric

1 teaspoon coriander

4 large fresh shrimp

For garnish

12 medium-sized shrimp

Pinch of salt

2 tablespoons olive oil

1/2 cup crushed almonds

In a small saucepan, sauté the onion in oil until soft. Add remaining soup ingredients and cook on low heat for 15 minutes. Puree well and keep on very low heat while you grill the shrimp for garnish.

Heat the grill to medium-high heat. Toss 12 shrimp with salt and olive oil. Grill for about 2 minutes per side. Ladle the soup into 6 bowls and top each bowl with two grilled shrimp and a sprinkle of crushed almonds.

Caldo Blanco

Chilled Almond and White Grape Gazpacho

A great surprise for people who say they don't like cold soups.

Serves 6

6 cloves garlic, whole

1/2 cup extra virgin olive oil

6 (1-inch-thick) baguette slices

2 cucumbers, peeled and diced

1/2 red onion, diced

2 cups whole green grapes

1 cup Marcona almonds

4 cups water

2 tablespoons sherry vinegar

1/4 cup amontillado sherry

Salt and freshly ground pepper

Cook the whole garlic cloves in olive oil over medium heat until
cooked through and browned. Remove the garlic cloves and set aside.
Toast the bread in the garlic-flavored oil for about 1 minute per side.
Place all ingredients in a blender and blend to a fine puree at high speed.
Chill the soup for 1 hour before serving.

Sopa de Yogur

Chilled Yogurt Soup

Perfect on a hot summer night served with Marinated Tomatoes (see page 40) and Moroccan Grilled Shrimp (see recipe on page 143)

Serves 6

2 cups plain yogurt

1/4 cup extra virgin olive oil

2 tablespoons lemon juice

2 cups milk

1/4 cup diced red onion

2 tablespoons chopped mint

1 red bell pepper, diced

2 tablespoons chopped fresh cilantro

1 teaspoon ground cumin

Mix all ingredients well in a blender. Serve in chilled bowls
or cocktail glasses.

Gazpacho de Sandia

Watermelon Gazpacho with Feta

This garden-fresh, raw, pureed cold soup is bursting with contrasting sweet, salty, and herbaceous flavors.

Serves 8

3 cups ½-inch-dice watermelon

3 small tomatoes

1 cup orange juice

½ cup extra virgin olive oil

1 large cucumber, chopped

1 red bell pepper, chopped

1 small red onion, chopped

3 cloves garlic

2 tablespoons sherry vinegar

3 tablespoons chopped fresh cilantro

2 thick slices bread

Salt and freshly ground black pepper

3 cups water

For garnish

2 cups crumbled feta

3 tablespoons fresh mint

2 tablespoons extra virgin olive oil

Place all ingredients in a large bowl and let sit for 10 minutes. Puree well and chill for 1–2 hours. Serve chilled with some crumbled feta, chopped mint, and a drizzle of olive oil on top of soup.

Sopa de Calabasa

Roasted Squash Bisque with Apples, Ham, and Mahon Cheese

On a chilly winter night, this might be all you need to cook. This would also be a great start to a roasted chicken dinner like Roasted Harissa Chicken (see page 206).

Serves 6

1 (2-pound) butternut squash
1 medium acorn squash
3 tablespoons butter
1 medium onion, finely chopped
4 cloves garlic, minced
1 tablespoon grated gingerroot
¼ cup sweet sherry
4 cups chicken stock
Salt and pepper to taste
1 tablespoon finely chopped fresh sage
1 cup half-and-half

Crostini

6 (½-inch thick) slices French baguette
4 tablespoons olive oil, divided
2 Granny Smith apples, peeled, cored, diced
½ pound smoked ham, diced
1 teaspoon finely chopped fresh sage
⅓ to ½ pound Mahon cheese

Preheat the oven to 350 degrees. Cut the squashes in half and scoop out the seeds. Place on a baking sheet cut side down and bake 1 to 1¼ hours, or until tender. Midway through baking, turn the squashes over to place the peel side down. Remove from the oven, but keep the temperature at 350 for the crostini. Scoop out the flesh and set aside. In large soup pot, melt the butter. Sauté the onion until soft. Stir in the garlic and gingerroot. Deglaze the pan with sherry. Stir in the stock and cooked squash. Season to taste with salt and pepper. Cook until the mixture boils; reduce the heat to simmer and cook about 15 minutes. Puree the soup, adding the sage and half-and-half. Keep warm.

For the crostini: Brush the bread slices with 2 tablespoons of the olive oil; place on a baking sheet. Bake 4 minutes at 350 degrees. In a medium-size sauté pan over medium heat, cook the apples, ham, and sage in the remaining oil until tender, about 3 minutes. Place 1 slice of cheese on each slice of bread, and top with a tablespoon of the apple-ham mixture.

Marmitako

Tuna and Potato Stew

This version of the classic Basque fisherman's stew has the tuna seared and placed on top instead of being cooked in the stew.

Serves 4

2 cups diced potatoes

Salt to taste, divided

1 red bell pepper, julienned

1 yellow onion, julienned

¼ cup plus 4 teaspoons olive oil, divided

1 teaspoon sherry vinegar

¼ cup Sofrito (see page 74)

1 teaspoon smoked hot paprika

1 cup fish stock

1 teaspoon chopped fresh thyme

Pepper to taste, divided

1 pound tuna, cut into 4 (4-ounce) pieces

Boil potatoes in salted water until soft; set aside. While potatoes are boiling, sauté the pepper and onion in ¼ cup olive oil with a little salt and the vinegar over low heat until caramelized, about 45 minutes. We like to cook this long and slow. Then add the cooked potatoes and all other ingredients except the tuna to the pepper-and-onion mixture. Cook for another 15 minutes.

Prepare 4 small plates. Place 3 tablespoons of the vegetable mixture on each plate. Adjust salt. Preheat a plancha or cast-iron skillet on high. Drizzle 1 teaspoon olive oil on each piece of tuna and sprinkle with salt and pepper. Sear tuna on the plancha for 1 minute per side. Serve on top of the vegetable mixture, one piece of tuna per plate.

Sopa de Bacalao

Bacalao and Potato Soup

Rich soup from the Basque region highlighting the versatility of the deceptively simple salt cod.

Serves 6

2 yellow onions, diced

4 cloves garlic, slivered

¼ cup extra virgin olive oil

1 pound salt cod (soaked in water for 24
   hours, changing the water 4 times)

1 quart fish stock

2 cups milk

¼ cup heavy cream

2 potatoes, diced

1 teaspoon salt

In a soup pot, sauté the onions and garlic in olive oil for 5 minutes on medium heat. Add remaining ingredients to the pot and bring to a boil. Turn down to low heat and let simmer for 20 minutes. Puree well and serve hot.

Sopa de Mejinnoes

Tomato-Fennel Fish Broth with Mussels

You'll love the classic Mediterranean flavor combinations of licorice fennel, sweet tomatoes, and briny mussels.

Serves 6

2 yellow onions, diced

2 ribs celery, diced

4 cloves garlic, slivered

2 fennel bulbs, cored and diced

1 red bell pepper, diced

4 carrots, peeled and diced

¼ cup extra virgin olive oil

1 cup white wine

Pinch of saffron

1 teaspoon salt

2 teaspoons black pepper

4 tomatoes, diced

6 cups fish stock

2 pounds fresh black mussels

In a soup pot over medium heat, sauté the onions, celery, garlic, fennel, bell pepper, and carrots in oil for 10 minutes. Add the wine and saffron and stir well. Add the salt, pepper, and tomatoes. Cook for 2 more minutes. Add the fish stock and bring to a boil. Add the mussels and cover. Cook for about 5 minutes, or until all the mussels pop open (discard those that don't open). Serve in bowls with spoons and seafood forks.

Vegetable Tapas

Queso de Cabra con Sofrito
Baked Goat Cheese with Sofrito

Hot, bubbling goat cheese with tomatoes and toasted bread. What could be better?

Serves 6

1/2 cup extra virgin olive oil, divided

18 (1/2-inch) slices of baguette

12 ounces fresh Spanish goat cheese

1/2 cup Sofrito (see below)

1/4 cup chopped fresh parsley

Heat the oven to 400 degrees. Heat 1/4 cup of the oil in a skillet over high heat. Add the bread slices and toast until slightly brown, about 1 minute per side. Set aside. Put the goat cheese in an ovenproof baking dish or cazuela and top with sofrito. Bake until hot and bubbly, about 8-10 minutes. When it comes out of the oven, drizzle the rest of the olive oil on top and sprinkle with parsley. Serve as a shared tapa with the toasted bread.

Sofrito

This is something to have on hand for use as a cooking ingredient in sauces, soups, and stews. The sofrito will give the dish a deep, slow-cooked, sweet vegetable flavor.

Makes 3 cups

4 large tomatoes, peeled and diced

1 green bell pepper or poblano
   pepper, seeded and diced

1 yellow onion, diced

1 clove garlic, minced

1/4 cup Spanish extra virgin olive oil

1 teaspoon pimenton

1 teaspoon Spanish sherry vinegar

Salt and pepper to taste

Heat the olive oil in a medium-size sauté pan. Add all other ingredients and cook on low heat for 35 minutes, until all ingredients are soft and well blended. Keep covered and refrigerated for up to 1 week.

Alcachofas

Grilled Artichokes with Goat Cheese, Orange, and Mint

Grilling the marinated artichokes burns off the harsh vinegar notes, giving them a new level of flavor.

Serves 6

6 medium-size artichokes
6 cloves garlic, slivered
½ cup lemon juice

Marinade

1 cup extra virgin olive oil
6 cloves garlic, minced
1 teaspoon salt
1 teaspoon black pepper
2 tablespoons lemon juice

For the plate

6 ounces fresh goat cheese
Chopped mint for garnish
Zest of 2 oranges
¼ cup extra virgin olive oil

Snip the points from the leaves of the artichokes and remove outer layer of leaves. Peel the stem and leave it attached (the stem has a lot of flavor but is often snipped off and thrown away). Cut the artichokes in half and boil them in water to cover, along with garlic and lemon juice, for about 20 minutes. Remove from the water and transfer to a bowl.

Mix the marinade ingredients and pour over warm artichokes. Allow to marinate at room temperature for 4 hours.

Heat a grill to medium-high heat. Grill the artichokes for about 3 minutes per side. Arrange 6 small plates with 2 grilled artichokes on each plate, along with a 1-ounce ball (about 2 tablespoons) of goat cheese. Sprinkle each plate with chopped mint, orange zest, and olive oil.

Berenjenas Parrillas

Grilled Eggplant with Melted Manchego, Capers, and Saffron Honey

This dish balances the sweetness of honey with the briny acidity of capers. The unmistakable flavor of saffron ties it all together.

Serves 6 as a first course

2 large eggplants, cut in 6 slices each

¼ cup olive oil

Salt and pepper to taste

Coarse salt and freshly ground black pepper

¼ pound shredded manchego cheese

2 tablespoons Saffron Honey (recipe follows)

2 teaspoons capers

Preheat a gas or charcoal grill to medium. Brush the eggplant slices lightly with olive oil and sprinkle with salt and pepper. Grill eggplant until tender, about 5 minutes per side. Transfer the eggplant from the grill to a cookie sheet and reduce the grill heat to low. (If using a charcoal grill, rake the majority of the coals to one side to create a cooler area.) Sprinkle each slice of eggplant with some manchego; then return the cookie sheet to the grill and lower the lid for about 5 minutes, just long enough for the cheese to melt. Plate the eggplant slices and drizzle each with Saffron Honey and sprinkle with capers. Serve warm.

Miel de Azafran
Saffron Honey

Stirring saffron threads into a little white wine helps to distribute the color and flavor of the spice throughout the honey.

Makes ¹/₂ cup

2 tablespoons white wine

¹/₂ teaspoon saffron threads

¹/₂ cup honey

In a small pan, heat the wine until it bubbles. Turn off the heat and stir in the saffron, then the honey. Use a rubber spatula to scrape the mixture into a glass jar and allow it to cool completely before putting on the lid.

Aguacates con Roncal
Avocados with Shaved Roncal and Olive Oil

This simple dish underscores the rich, velvety texture of the avocados. Roncal, a cured sheep's milk cheese, adds a sharp, tangy flavor all its own.

Serves 6

3 ripe avocados

¹/₄ cup Spanish extra virgin olive oil

Sea salt to taste

¹/₄ pound Roncal cheese

Cut each avocado in half and peel. Each plate will get half an avocado sliced into 4 pieces. On each plate of avocados, drizzle 2 teaspoons olive oil, sprinkle with salt, and shave about 1 ounce cheese on top using a vegetable peeler.

Alcaparonnes

Fried Caperberries

Caperberries are popular in Spain and are eaten like olives, right out of the jar. This recipe turns them into a crispy, salty bar snack that should have a glass of chilled fino sherry served with it.

Serves 6

4 cups olive oil

1 large jar caperberries (about 30 pieces)

4 egg whites, blended

2 cups flour

Heat the oil in a deep pan until hot. Dip the caperberries in egg whites and then roll in flour. Deep-fry in three batches (10 pieces at a time). Transfer to a plate lined with paper towels. Serve hot. They don't need salt.

Escalivada

Roasted Vegetables

This is a colorful, classic-style roasted vegetable dish. Try adding some different colors of peppers and tomatoes from a farmers market. This dish pairs well with purchased boquerones (pickled anchovies) or Pinchos de Boquerone y Romesco (see page 120).

Serves 4

2 red bell peppers

1 green chile (Anaheim or poblano)

1 medium eggplant, sliced

1 zucchini, halved lengthwise

2 small red onions, sliced

4 Roma tomatoes, halved

6 cloves garlic, peeled

1/2 cup extra virgin olive oil,
   plus more for drizzling

3 tablespoons sherry vinegar

Salt and ground black pepper

Heat the oven to 375 degrees. Toss all ingredients together in a large bowl and then transfer to a baking sheet. Roast for about 30 minutes, until the vegetables are well cooked and tender. Allow to cool. Peel the eggplant and peppers and remove the stems and seeds. Cut all the cooked vegetables into 2-inch strips and arrange in a colorful pattern on 4 small plates. Drizzle with a little more olive oil and serve at room temperature.

Esparrogos Olivada

Grilled Asparagus with Olivada

Try this on your outdoor grill the next time you cook steak.

Serves 6

2 bundles (about 1½ pounds)
   green asparagus

4 quarts water

1 teaspoon sea salt plus more to taste

Juice of 2 lemons

¼ cup olive oil

2 tablespoons Olivada (recipe follows)

Fire up a gas or charcoal grill to medium-high heat. Trim 1 inch from the cut end of the asparagus. Prepare an ice bath large enough to accommodate the asparagus (half ice and half cold water). Bring water to a boil and add 1 teaspoon salt. Blanch asparagus by dropping into the boiling water for 2 minutes and then transfer to the ice bath. Remove the asparagus from the ice bath and toss in a bowl with salt, lemon juice, and olive oil. Grill for about 2 minutes. Transfer asparagus to 6 small plates and top with Olivada.

Olivada

Black Olive Paste

Makes about 1 cup

1 cup black olives, pitted

3 cloves garlic

½ cup olive oil

½ cup parsley

1 tablespoon capers

1 tablespoon Sofrito (see page 74)

Blend all ingredients well with a mortar and pestle or food processor. Refrigerate covered for up to 1 week.

Esparragos Blancos

White Asparagus in Sherry Vinaigrette, Oranges, and Parsley

Spaniards love these white asparagus, which are grown in darkness to prevent the production of chlorophyll. Unlike most vegetables, the canned variety is very good and could be substituted nicely in this recipe.

Serves 6

Salt to taste, divided

2 bunches white asparagus, peeled

$1/2$ cup extra virgin olive oil

3 tablespoons sherry vinegar

$1/4$ cup chopped parsley

Black pepper to taste

2 oranges, sectioned

Bring 2 quarts of water to a boil with 2 teaspoons of salt. Cook the asparagus for 4 minutes and then drain. Transfer asparagus to a large plate while still warm. Whisk together the olive oil, vinegar, parsley, salt to taste, and pepper to taste. Pour the dressing over the asparagus. Top with orange sections.

Revueltos

Scrambled Eggs with Asparagus and Manchego on Toasts

A simple scrambled egg dish celebrates the spring asparagus in a very Spanish way.

Serves 6

¹/₂ cup Spanish extra virgin olive oil, divided

12 (1-inch-thick) baguette slices

1 bunch green asparagus (1 inch
   trimmed from cut end)

¹/₂ yellow onion, diced

6 eggs, beaten and seasoned
   lightly with salt and pepper

¹/₄ pound manchego cheese, shredded

Heat ¹/₄ cup olive oil in a sauté pan on high heat. Add the bread slices
and toast until slightly brown, about 1 minute per side. Transfer toasts
to six plates (2 per plate). Add remaining olive oil to the pan. Add
asparagus and onion and sauté for 3 minutes. Add eggs and stir until
cooked. Stir in the cheese and remove from heat. Spoon equal amounts
of asparagus-and-egg mixture on top of each toast.

Cazuela de Espinaca

Baked Spinach with Goat Cheese and Onion-Raisin Compota

A classic cheese and fruit combination offsets the earthy flavors of the spinach.

Makes about 2 cups

Baked Spinach

¼ cup olive oil

1 cup baby spinach leaves

4 cloves garlic, slivered

6 ounces fresh Spanish goat cheese

Heat the oven to 400 degrees. Heat olive oil in a large sauté pan. Sauté the spinach and garlic for about 3 minutes. Divide spinach into 6 *cazuelas* (small terra-cotta dishes). Top each *cazuela* of spinach with 1 ounce (2 tablespoons) goat cheese and a spoonful of Onion-Raisin Compota. Bake in the oven for 5 minutes, until cheese is bubbly. Serve hot.

Serves 6

Onion-Raisin Compota

½ onion, chopped

3 tablespoons olive oil

2 cups golden raisins

3 tablespoons honey

¼ cup oloroso sherry

1 teaspoon salt

Sauté the onion in olive oil until soft. Add remaining ingredients and simmer for 5 minutes. Remove from heat and set aside.

Pincho de Huevo

Egg Bruschetta with Mushrooms and Truffle Oil

So simple, so good. I like to call this dish "eggs and toast."

Serves 6

½ cup extra virgin olive oil, divided

6 (1-inch) baguette slices

1 pound mushrooms, sliced

3 cloves garlic, minced

2 teaspoons chopped fresh sage

1 cup heavy cream

½ cup shredded manchego cheese

1 teaspoon salt

2 teaspoons cracked black pepper

6 eggs

4 teaspoons truffle oil

Heat ¼ cup olive oil in a sauté pan on high heat. Add the bread slices and toast until slightly brown, about 1 minute per side. Set aside. Heat remaining olive oil in the pan, and sauté the mushrooms with garlic and sage.

Heat the cream in a large sauté pan on medium heat. Add the toasted bread and sautéed mushrooms to the cream. Cook for 5 minutes. Turn the bread over gently. Cook for 3 more minutes and add the cheese, salt, and pepper. Turn off heat. Lay out 6 small plates. Transfer a bread slice to each plate and top with equal amounts of the mushroom cream.

Fry 6 eggs over easy and top each dish with a fried egg. Drizzle each dish with a teaspoon of truffle oil.

Betabeles

Roasted Beets

Rich, earthy roasted beets become more lively with the bright flavors of Southern Spain.

Serves 6

2 pounds red or golden beets,
  washed and trimmed

¼ cup olive oil

¼ cup Spanish sherry vinegar

Salt and pepper to taste

3 oranges, cut into peeled segments

1 teaspoon ground cumin seeds

3 ounces (6 tablespoons) soft
  Spanish goat cheese

Heat the oven to 375 degrees. Put beets in a roasting pan and toss with
olive oil, vinegar, salt, and pepper. Roast until cooked through, about
45 minutes. Cut beets into 8 wedges each. Divide pieces evenly among
6 plates. Top each plate of beets with orange segments, a sprinkle of
cumin and 1 tablespoon goat cheese.

Alborina

Roasted Autumn Vegetables and Peppers

This kind of hearty, winter ratatouille for colder weather vegetables goes nicely with a main dish of lamb.

Serves 6

1 pound butternut squash,
 peeled and cubed

$^1/_2$ pound tomatoes, cut in wedges

1 red bell pepper, cut into 1-inch dice

1 poblano pepper, cut into 1-inch dice

1 bay leaf

8 cloves garlic

1 onion, chopped

2 cups cooked garbanzos

$^1/_2$ cup extra virgin olive oil

2 large potatoes, cubed

1 teaspoon salt

2 teaspoons cracked black pepper

Place all the ingredients on a sheet pan and roast for 45 minutes.
Discard the bay leaf and serve from the baking dish.

Manchego Frito

Fried Manchego Cheese

This fries up like a cheese tempura. It can be served with a few slices of membrillo *paste,* **or dulce de membrillo,** *or guava paste.*

Serves 6

1 egg

1 cup ice water

1 cup sifted all-purpose flour

Vegetable oil for deep-frying

6 ounces manchego cheese,

   cut into 12 pieces

Beat the egg in a bowl and add ice water (be sure it is very cold).

Add sifted flour and mix lightly. Be careful not to overmix the batter.

Heat oil to 350 degrees in a deep fryer or other heavy-bottomed pan.

Dip each piece of cheese into batter and fry until golden brown,

about 45 seconds.

Paté de Hongos

Mushroom Paté with Roasted Garlic and Oloroso

I like to serve this vegetarian paté with some freshly baked bread. The oloroso sherry lends a subtle sweet nuttiness to the dish.

Serves 6

½ cup olive oil

15 cloves garlic

1 yellow onion, diced

1 pound crimini mushrooms, sliced

1 pound button mushrooms, sliced

Salt and black pepper to taste

1 tablespoon whole grain Dijon mustard

2 tablespoons parsley

1 tablespoon sage

¼ cup oloroso sherry

4 green onions, chopped

Heat the olive oil in a small skillet on medium heat. Add the garlic cloves and cook for 8 minutes, until light brown and cooked through; set pan aside to cool. Remove garlic with a slotted spoon. Transfer the garlic-flavored oil to a larger sauté pan. Turn up the heat to high and sauté the onion until soft, about 4 minutes. Add all of the mushrooms, salt, and pepper, and sauté for about 10 minutes, until soft. Add mustard, parsley, sage, garlic, and sherry and cook for 10 more minutes. Turn off heat and allow mixture to cool. Puree well in a food processor then transfer mixture to six 2-ounce ramekins. Cool in the refrigerator for at least 1 hour. When ready to serve, garnish each dish with a small amount of chopped green onion.

Ñoquis en Salsa de Cabrales

Potato Gnocchi in Blue Cheese Cream with Porcini Mushrooms

Inspired by Italian pasta making, this rich, creamy blue cheese tapa could be followed by a grilled tomato salad for a simple lunch.

Serves 6

¼ cup extra virgin olive oil

4 large porcini mushrooms,
   cleaned and sliced

2 cloves garlic, slivered

2 tablespoons chopped sage

1 teaspoon salt

¼ cup white wine

Potato Gnocchi

1 pound potatoes, peeled
   and cut into quarters

3 eggs, beaten

2 tablespoons olive oil

Salt to taste

1 cup flour

Blue Cheese Cream

3 tablespoons butter

2 cups heavy cream

3 ounces Cabrales cheese

Heat the olive oil in a skillet and sauté the mushrooms with garlic, sage, and salt for about 4 minutes. Add the wine and cook for another 2 minutes. Set aside.

To make the gnocchi: Boil potatoes for about 15 minutes, until soft; drain and allow to cool to room temperature. Push the potatoes through a ricer into a mixing bowl. Add eggs, olive oil, salt, and flour, and mix with a wooden spoon until a dough forms. Form dough into six balls. Roll each ball with your hands into a long rope about 1 inch in diameter. Heat a pot of water to boiling. Cut dough ropes into ½-inch pieces. Boil the gnocchi until they float, about 1 minute.

To make the blue cheese cream: Heat butter in a large sauté pan over medium-high heat. Remove gnocchi from water with a slotted spoon and transfer to the sauté pan; brown the gnocchi for about 2 minutes. Add the cream and reduce for 4 minutes. Add the cheese and remove from heat. Transfer to a large platter, top with the sautéed mushrooms, and share with friends.

Salmorejo

Thick Tomato Bread Puree

A simple dish packed with flavor, this thick puree is somewhere between a gazpacho and a vegetable spread and is enjoyed throughout the Iberian Peninsula.

Serves 4

1¼ cups extra virgin olive oil, divided

4 (1-inch) slices of baguette

2 ripe tomatoes

4 cloves garlic

½ tablespoon sherry vinegar

Chopped hardboiled egg, for garnish

Fried jamón serrano, for garnish

Tuna, good-quality canned,
   for garnish (optional)

Heat a skillet with ¼ cup olive oil, and toast the bread until brown and crispy on both sides. Set aside to cool. Put all ingredients into a blender, and blend until a smooth, thick puree is formed. Chill for one hour. Serve garnished with chopped hardboiled egg and fried jamón serrano, or good-quality canned tuna and olive oil.

Pipérade

Red Pepper Stew

This classic from the Basque country is great spooned over eggs or in an omelet.

Makes 10 servings

2 tablespoons extra virgin olive oil

1 yellow onion, diced

1 green bell pepper, julienned

2 red bell peppers, julienned

2 cloves garlic, minced

1/2 teaspoon salt

1/4 teaspoon smoked paprika

Black pepper to taste

2 cups diced tomatoes

Heat the olive oil in a large skillet over medium heat. Sauté the onion, peppers, and garlic sprinkled with salt, paprika, and black pepper. Cook for 10 minutes, stirring frequently, until the vegetables are cooked through. Add the tomatoes to the cooked vegetables and simmer the mixture uncovered for 15 minutes, until most of the liquid has evaporated and the sauce has thickened.

Piquillos Confitados

Piquillo-Garlic Confit with Shaved Idiazabal

A few simple ingredients can make a memorable tapa. The piquillos are slowly steeped in Spanish extra virgin olive oil with garlic and topped with the slightly smoky Idiazabal cheese from the Basque country.

Serves 4

2 cups piquillo peppers, cut in strips

6 whole cloves garlic

1 cup extra virgin olive oil

Salt

2 ounces Idiazabal cheese

Cook peppers and garlic in olive oil on low heat for 1 hour.
Add salt to taste. Drain and reserve oil. Serve the peppers
and garlic warm with a drizzle of the cooking oil and shaved cheese.
(Conserve the garlic-pepper-flavored oil for other uses).

Hummus

Garbanzo-Carrot Hummus with Grilled Yogurt Flatbread

This is a lively hummus spiked with Moroccan flavors. Grilled yogurt flatbread, similar to the naan you find in Indian restaurants, is one of the easiest breads to make.

Makes 2 cups

2 medium carrots, peeled and chopped

Salt

1 cup cooked garbanzo beans, drained

4 teaspoons chopped cilantro plus
  1 teaspoon for garnish

2 tablespoons chopped red onion

2½ teaspoons ground cumin

1½ teaspoons ground coriander seeds

2 tablespoons lemon juice

4 teaspoons olive oil

2 teaspoons chile flakes

2 teaspoons Moroccan Spice Blend
  (see page 104)

Coarse salt and freshly ground black pepper

1 batch Yogurt Flatbread (recipe follows)

In a medium saucepan, combine the carrots with 2 quarts water and 2 teaspoons salt. Bring the mixture to a boil then reduce the heat and simmer for 8–10 minutes, until the carrots are tender. Remove the pan from the heat and allow the carrots to drain and cool in a colander.

Combine carrots and remaining ingredients, except for Yogurt Flatbread, in the work bowl of a food processor and puree until smooth. Season to taste with salt and pepper and garnish with the remaining cilantro. Serve with fresh, hot Yogurt Flatbread cut in wedges.

> continued

Moroccan Spice Blend

This spice rub is also great for grilled shrimp or pork skewers. Simply grind a few cloves of garlic with a mortar and pestle and add the spice blend, a little salt, a splash of lemon juice, and 2 splashes of olive oil.

Makes about 2 tablespoons

1 teaspoon ground cumin

1 teaspoon ground turmeric

1 teaspoon saffron threads

1 teaspoon ground coriander

1 teaspoon ground cinnamon

1 teaspoon ground smoked paprika

1 teaspoon finely grated lemon peel

In a small resealable glass or plastic container, combine all of the ingredients.

Pan de Yogur
Yogurt Flatbread

Serves 4

1 cup all-purpose flour

1/4 teaspoon baking powder

1 teaspoon coarse salt

2 1/2 cups plain yogurt

Olive oil

Sift the flour, baking powder and salt into the work bowl of a stand mixer fitted with the dough hook. Add the yogurt and mix on low speed (setting 2 on a KitchenAid) for 2 minutes. Cover the work bowl and allow the dough to rest at room temperature for 30 minutes.

Preheat a gas or charcoal grill to medium. Scrape the dough from the work bowl and turn it out onto a lightly floured surface. Roll the dough into a long log and divide it into 12 equal pieces. Roll each piece into a ball and use a rolling pin or tortilla press to flatten it into a 1/4-inch-thick tortilla shape. Brush each "tortilla" lightly with olive oil. Grill each for about 40 seconds then turn and cook another 40 seconds.

Mozzarella Parrilla

Grilled Mozzarella Skewers

A simple summer grilled tapa bursting with contrasting Mediterranean flavors of grapes, olives, caperberries, and fresh mozzarella.

Serves 6

1 cup extra virgin olive oil

2 tablespoons Spanish sherry vinegar

1 tablespoon fresh lemon juice

1 tablespoon chopped fresh oregano

1 teaspoon crushed red pepper flakes

2 teaspoons minced garlic

12 fresh mozzarella ciliegine
   balls (1/3 ounce each)

12 seedless red grapes

12 pitted kalamata olives

12 cherry tomatoes

12 large caperberries, plus more for garnish

6 (8-inch) to 12 (6-inch) skewers

Olivada (see page 84)

Lemon wedges for garnish

In a large bowl, mix the oil, vinegar, lemon juice, oregano, pepper flakes, and garlic. Add the remaining ingredients except Olivada and lemon wedges; toss well to coat. Refrigerate for 2 hours to marinate.

Heat a gas or charcoal grill to medium.

For 8-inch skewers, thread 1 mozzarella ball, 1 grape, 1 olive, 1 tomato, and 1 caperberry on each skewer; repeat so you have two of each item on a skewer. For 6-inch skewers, thread 1 of each item, in the same order. Grill the skewers on all sides for 5 to 7 minutes, or until the cheese is soft. Serve the skewers as a tapa or a side to grilled meat. To serve, transfer the skewers to a serving platter. Top with Olivada. Garnish with lemon wedges and caperberries.

Pisto Manchego

Vegetable Stew with Fried Egg

This rich stew of harvest vegetables—eggplant, zucchini, onions, tomatoes, and garlic—makes a great rustic lunch with a fried egg on top and a salad on the side.

Serves 4

¼ cup Spanish olive oil

1 large yellow onion, diced

2 medium eggplants, peeled
   and cut into 1-inch pieces

2 large zucchini, cut into 1-inch pieces
   (about 2 cups)

2 green bell peppers or poblanos,
   seeded and diced

6 cloves garlic, peeled

4 large ripe tomatoes, diced

2 teaspoons sherry vinegar

Salt and pepper to taste

4 fried eggs

Heat the olive oil in a sauté pan over medium heat. Sauté the eggplant and onion together until the onion is translucent, about 5 minutes. Add zucchini, peppers, and garlic. Sauté slowly until all ingredients have softened. Add tomatoes and stir. Cover and cook on medium heat for 10–15 minutes, stirring frequently. Add the vinegar and salt and pepper to taste. Simmer over low heat for 40 minutes, stirring occasionally and adding small amounts of water if necessary. The zucchini and eggplant should be very soft. Serve in bowls and top each with a fried egg.

Pimientos Rellenos

Green Chiles Stuffed with Cheese

Pimientos de pardon, small green chiles from the Galicia region, have been showing up in farmers markets all over the United States. They are picked young and do not need to be peeled. Some are hot and some are not!

Serves 6

36 pimientos de pardon

36 small cubes of cow's milk cheese,
  such as Spanish Mahon or Tetilla

¼ cup Spanish extra virgin olive oil

2 teaspoons sea salt

Cut an opening in each chile long enough to place the cheese cube into. After filling, squeeze the chile to close the opening as much as possible.

Heat a large sauté pan or cast-iron skillet to medium-high heat, and heat the olive oil. Working in batches, cook the chiles with a sprinkling of sea salt until they are slightly browned and the cheese is melted. This will take about 2–3 minutes. Transfer to small plates and enjoy with a pint of beer.

Seafood
Tapas

Cataplana

Clam Stew in a Copper Pot

Cataplana is the name of a rustic-looking hammered copper pot that is hinged like a clamshell. All the ingredients and cooking liquid are secured inside with a clasp. The whole pot is cooked in the oven or over an open flame until the clams pop open.

Serves 6

1½ pounds fresh clams

2 cups diced tomatoes

1 yellow onion, diced

6 cloves garlic, slivered

1 cup diced red bell peppers

2 cups fish stock

1 cup Spanish Alborino wine

3 tablespoons chopped parsley

1 teaspoon salt

4 tablespoons extra virgin olive oil

Heat oven to 400 degrees. Combine all ingredients and place in a cataplana or a small Dutch oven with a lid. Put in the oven for 15–20 minutes. The clams will steam open inside. Remove from the oven and carefully remove lid; the escaping steam will be very hot. Divide the clams and the juices into 6 small bowls. Serve hot.

Gambas Andaluz

Fried Shrimp

Simple fried fish calls out for a chilled Manzanilla sherry. Try this batter on any seafood, especially cod, oysters, and scallops. A mixed platter would be a great variation.

Serves 6

4 cups olive oil

24 large shrimp, peeled and deveined

12 egg whites (2 cups), blended

2 cups flour

Sea salt to taste

Heat the olive oil in a deep pot on medium-high heat for 10 minutes, until it reaches 300–350 degrees.

Dip the shrimp 3 at a time into the egg whites and then into the flour. Place directly into the hot oil, being careful not to splash. Deep-fry for about 1 minute. Remove from the oil with a slotted spoon and place on a plate lined with paper towels. Sprinkle with sea salt and serve while hot.

Bonito Crudo

Tuna Carpaccio

A bit more of a modern-style raw tuna tapa, this is great when paired with a fino sherry.

Serves 4

12 ounces raw tuna loin

1 cup chopped black olives

1 tablespoon smoked sea salt

1/2 cup Pickled Red Onion (see page 33)

1/4 cup Blood Orange Aioli

Slice the tuna into very thin slices and lay out on a chilled platter. Top with olives, a sprinkle of sea salt, pickled onions, and Blood Orange Aioli. Serve chilled.

Blood Orange Aioli

Makes 1/4 cup

1 egg yolk

1 teaspoon lemon juice

1 clove garlic

Pinch of sea salt

4 tablespoons olive oil

2 tablespoons blood orange juice

Using a stick blender, blend the egg yolk with the lemon juice, garlic, and salt. Then add the olive oil slowly while the blender is running. Add the blood orange juice and blend.

Esparrogos con Salmone

Asparagus with Smoked Salmon and Goat Cheese

Spring asparagus is great on the grill. Try stuffing one of these bundles into an omelet, along with the goat cheese.

Serves 6

2 bundles green asparagus

2 teaspoons sea salt, divided

1 tablespoon lemon juice

¼ cup extra virgin olive oil
   plus more for drizzling

6 slices smoked salmon

6 ounces fresh Spanish goat cheese

1 tablespoon capers

Pepper

Fire up a gas or charcoal grill to medium-high heat. Trim 1 inch from the cut end of each asparagus spear. Prepare an ice bath large enough to accommodate the asparagus (half ice and half cold water). In a large saucepan, bring water to a boil, enough to cover the asparagus; add 1 teaspoon sea salt. Blanch asparagus by setting it in the boiling water for 2 minutes; then transfer to ice bath. Remove the asparagus from the ice bath into a bowl and toss with remaining sea salt, lemon juice, and most of the olive oil. Grill for about 2 minutes. Wrap 3 spears asparagus with a slice of smoked salmon and repeat this 5 more times. Put each bundle on a small plate with 1 ounce (about 2 tablespoons) goat cheese, a few capers, and a drizzle of olive oil.

Pinchos de Boquerone y Romesco

Olive Oil Toasts with Pickled Anchovies and Romesco Sauce

*Romesco is a rich, velvety blend of almonds, garlic, roasted red peppers, and olive oil.
It is a versatile sauce. With the acidity of the anchovies, this pairing is mysteriously simple
and exotic at the same time.*

Serves 6

½ cup olive oil

12 (1-inch) baguette slices

2 cups Romesco Sauce (see page 149)

24 boquerones (white anchovies)

Heat the olive oil in a large skillet over medium-high heat. Toast the
bread for about 2 minutes per side. Top each slice with 1 tablespoon
Salsa Romesco and 2 boquerones. Serve on a platter and share.

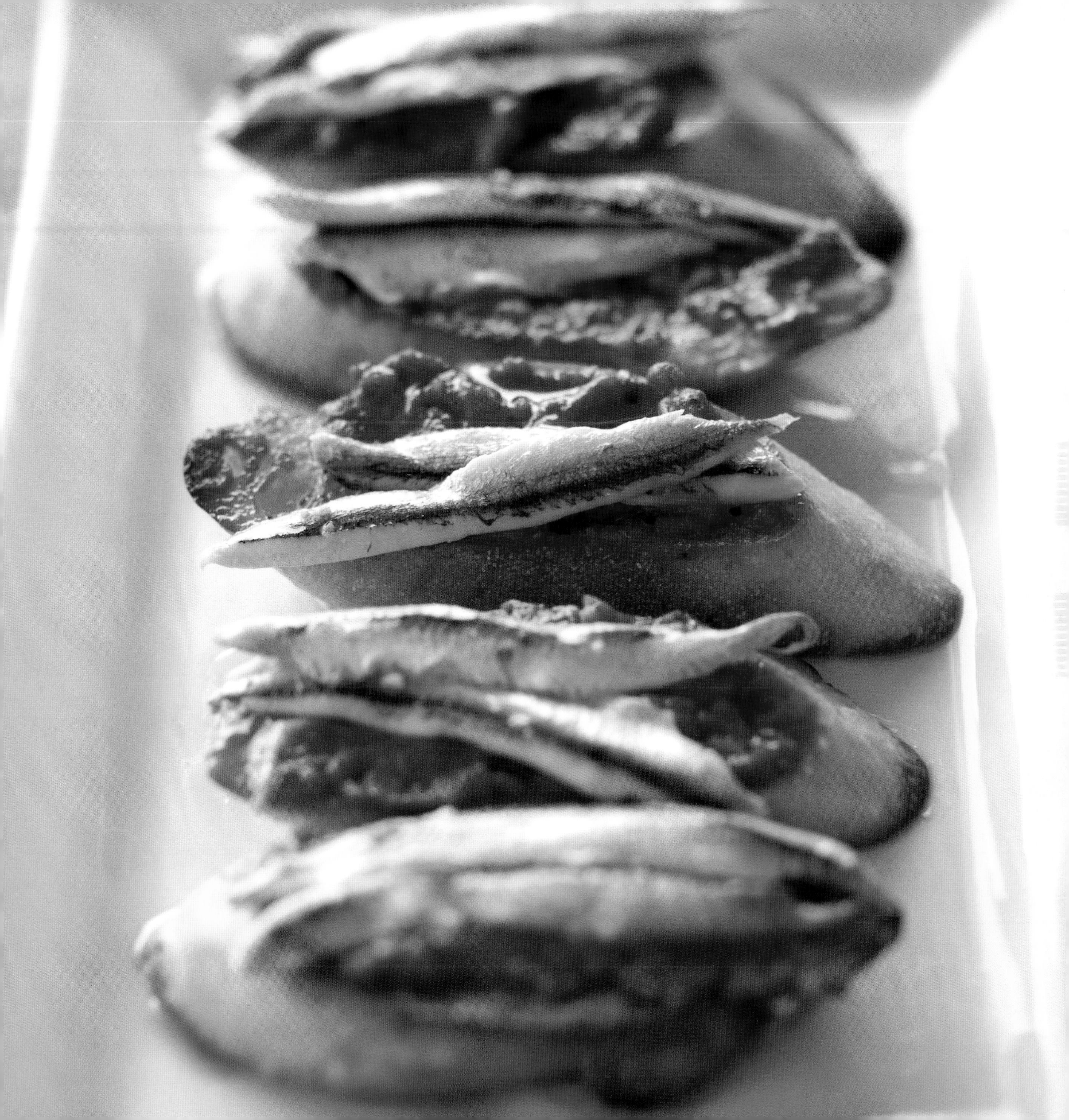

Pulpo en Vinegretta

Octopus in Vinaigrette

Octopus is everywhere in Spain. It is inexpensive, easy to cook, and delicious.

Serves 6

2 large octopuses

1 cup red wine

8 cups water

2 bay leaves

1 yellow onion, quartered

4 cloves garlic, crushed

1 tablespoon salt, plus more to taste

2 tablespoons lemon juice

2 tablespoons chopped parsley

$\frac{1}{2}$ cup extra virgin olive oil

In a large saucepan, combine all ingredients except the lemon juice, parsley, and olive oil, and cook on low heat for 2 hours. Allow the octopus to cool to room temperature in the cooking liquid. Cut all of the octopus into thin slices and transfer to a large platter. Dress the octopus with lemon juice, parsley, olive oil, and a pinch of salt. Let stand for 20 minutes before serving.

Calamares a la Plancha

Grilled Squid with Squid Ink and Piquillo Pepper Puree

Searing the little squid on hot iron gives it a more pronounced flavor than fried versions. Paint your plate with colorful black and red sauces of squid ink and piquillo pepper.

Serves 6

2 pounds baby squid with tentacles, cleaned

1/4 cup extra virgin olive oil

2 teaspoons sea salt

2 tablespoons lemon juice

4 cloves garlic, minced

4 piquillo peppers

2 tablespoons squid ink*

Toss the squid with olive oil, salt, lemon juice, and garlic. Marinate for 30 minutes. Heat a cast-iron skillet or flat grill plancha to high heat. Puree the peppers well in a blender. This puree will be used as one of the sauces. Grill the squid for about 2 minutes per side. Remove from heat and divide onto 6 small plates. Drizzle a small amount of squid ink and red pepper puree onto each plate.

Can be found in specialty stores such as the Spanish Table and La Tienda.com.

Pulpo Frito

Crispy Fried Octopus with Salmon Roe Aioli and Pickled Green Chiles

We like the classic combination of quickly fried salty seafood with Manzanilla. The brininess of the salmon roe aioli will enhance and bring forward the great "ocean spray" quality of the wine. We always like something pickled with fried foods for balance of fat and vinegar flavors. The vinegar aspect of the pickle with the dryness of the Manzanilla also creates a nice balance on the tongue, like an olive in a martini, for example.

Serves 4

1 large octopus, cleaned

½ yellow onion, chopped

3 cloves garlic, chopped

1 small tomato, chopped

2 teaspoons salt

2 teaspoons pimenton (Spanish paprika)

4 cups water

4 cups Manzanilla sherry

1 wine cork*

Salmon Roe Aioli (see page 128)

Pickled Green Chiles (see page 128)

Bring all ingredients (except aioli and pickled chiles) to a boil in a large saucepan. Turn down to low heat and cover. Let cook for 2 hours, or until octopus is very tender. Allow to cool and then separate legs from the body. We will fry the 8 legs; save the rest of the body for other uses or discard.

*The wine cork makes the octopus tenderer. It is and old European technique that I learned somewhere along the way. I do not know how or why it works; I only know when I don't use it, the octopus is not as tender.

> continued

Salmon Roe Aioli

Makes about 1 cup

1 egg yolk

Juice of 1/2 lemon (about 1 tablespoon)

2 cloves garlic, minced

Salt and pepper to taste

1 tablespoon salmon roe

1/2 cup extra virgin olive oil

1/2 cup canola oil

1 teaspoon pimenton

With a mortar and pestle, blend the yolk with lemon juice, garlic, salt, pepper, and roe. Add the oils slowly until the aioli thickens. Stir in pimenton.

Pickled Green Chiles

1 cup water

1 cup white wine vinegar

1 bay leaf

1 teaspoon dry oregano

2 tablespoons salt

1 teaspoon ground black pepper

4 tablespoons sugar

Juice of 1/2 orange (1 tablespoon)

2 New Mexico green or poblano chiles, julienned

1/4 red onion, julienned

Combine all ingredients except the chiles and onions in a small saucepan. Bring to a boil for 1 minute. Remove from heat and pour into a bowl with the chiles and onions. Allow to marinate and cool to room temperature. Refrigerate for 2 hours. Strain, discarding the liquid, and use the chiles and onions for the dish.

Fried Octopus

Serves 4

1 quart vegetable oil

3 cups rice flour

2 teaspoons sea salt, divided

3 cups egg whites

2 teaspoons sea salt, divided

Heat the oil in a large pot to 350 degrees. Mix flour with 1 teaspoon sea salt. Dip octopus legs in egg whites and then in the flour-salt mixture. Deep-fry until crispy and golden (about 30 seconds). Remove from oil and sprinkle with remaining salt. Serve 2 legs per plate as soon as they are fried, while still hot. Place 1 tablespoon of Pickled Green Chiles on the plate next to the octopus and spoon 2 tablespoons of chilled Salmon Roe Aioli on the side for dipping.

Puré de Bacaloa

Salt Cod Puree with Egg and Toast

Bacalao is salt cod, preserved and re-hydrated 24 hours prior to cooking. In this version, it is pureed with potatoes and onion for a smooth spread on olive oil toasts.

Serves 6

1 pound salt cod bacalao (see page 25)

1 pound Yukon gold potatoes, diced

1 yellow onion, julienned

4 cups milk

6 whole cloves garlic

Salt to taste

$\frac{1}{2}$ cup olive oil

Oil for frying

6 eggs

A day in advance, prepare the salt cod.

Preheat oven to 350 degrees. Put all ingredients except the oils and eggs in a medium saucepan. Bring to a boil and then turn down to a low simmer for 30 minutes, or until potatoes are tender. Allow to cool slightly then transfer this mixture to a food processor. Add the olive oil and blend well. Check seasoning and add salt if needed. Transfer to six small baking dishes or cazuelas. Bake in oven for 20 minutes.

On the stovetop in a large skillet, heat the oil and fry the eggs over easy. For each serving, place 1 egg on top of the cod mixture. Serve with crusty bread.

Gambas a la Plancha
Flat-Grilled Shrimp with Pimenton and Shaved Marcona Almonds

This great tapas bar dish is made rich with shaved Marcona almonds. The plancha is a flat iron grill. A good cast-iron pan is a great substitute.

Serves 6

1/2 cup olive oil

Juice of 1 lemon

2 teaspoons sea salt

24 medium-large shrimp (about 1 pound),
   in the shell with heads intact

10 Marcona almonds

In a bowl, whisk together the olive oil, lemon juice, and salt until well blended. Heat a plancha, grill, or cast-iron skillet to high heat. Toss the shrimp in the oil-lemon mixture.

Working in batches, grill the shrimp in a single layer without crowding. Sear for 1 minute. Decrease the heat to medium and continue cooking for 1 minute longer. Turn the shrimp, increase the heat to high, and sear for 2 more minutes, or until shrimp are golden. Keep the shrimp warm on an ovenproof platter in a low oven. Cook the rest of the shrimp in the same way.

When all the shrimp are cooked, arrange on a platter and serve immediately. Using a microplane or fine cheese grater, grind the almonds over the shrimp and let the almond dust sprinkle down.

Pinchos de Cangrejo

Crab Salad Toasts

Pinchos are tapas served in San Sebastian that are often in the form of toasted bread with an endless variety of toppings.

Serves 6

1 pound cooked crabmeat

3 tablespoons mayonnaise

Juice of ¹/₂ lemon (1 tablespoon)

Salt

1 teaspoon pimenton (Spanish paprika)

2 tablespoons chopped parsley

¹/₄ cup olive oil

12 (¹/₂-inch-thick) baguette toasts

2 ripe avocados, cut into 6 slices each

Mix first six ingredients in a bowl. Heat the oil in a skillet. Place the baguette slices in the hot oil and toast on both sides. Top each slice with 1 tablespoon of crab salad and 1 slice of avocado.

Pinchos de Bonito y Idiazabal

Tuna Toasts with Melted Idiazabal

These are like mini tuna melts with the artisanal cheese Idiazabal, a slightly smoky sheep's milk cheese from the Basque country that is eaten in great quantities.

Serves 6

1/2 red onion, finely diced

1/2 cup chopped kalamata olives

1/2 cup mayonnaise

1 tablespoon lemon juice

3 tablespoons parsley chopped

1/2 cup extra virgin olive oil, divided

1 red bell pepper, roasted,
   peeled, and chopped

1 (16-ounce) can tuna in olive oil, drained

12 (1/2-inch) baguette slices

12 small, thin slices Idiazabal cheese

In a bowl, mix all ingredients together except baguette and cheese—using just 1/4 cup of the olive oil—and refrigerate for 1 hour.

Heat the oven to 350 degrees. Heat the remaining 1/4 cup olive oil in a skillet. Place baguette slices in the hot oil and toast on both sides. Top each toast with 2 tablespoons of tuna salad. Top each *pincho* with a slice of cheese. Transfer to a baking sheet and cook for 45 minutes. Transfer to a large platter and share.

Boquerones con Queso

White Anchovies Stuffed with Goat Cheese

The little pickled white anchovies have a nice, firm texture for rolling and stuffing. Try some other fillings, such as chopped arugula, cherry tomatoes, fresh figs, or ham-stuffed olives.

Serves 4

4 ounces Spanish goat cheese

16 marinated white anchovies

Extra virgin olive oil

Zest of 2 oranges

Roll goat cheese into 16 marble-sized balls. Wrap each ball with an anchovy and secure with a skewer or toothpick. Serve on a platter with a drizzle of olive oil and a sprinkle of orange zest.

Langosta Cus Cus

Lobster with Saffron Couscous, Idiazabal, and Piquillos

This is a creamy "mac and cheese" type dish that you can be proud to serve.

Serves 4

2 pounds lobster meat

3 tablespoons butter

Pinch of saffron

1 cup heavy cream

1 pound cooked Israeli couscous

1 cup shredded Idiazabal cheese

4 piquillo peppers, julienned

Salt and pepper to taste

Sauté lobster meat in butter and saffron. Add the cream and couscous. Cook on medium heat until hot and the cream is partially reduced. Add the cheese and peppers and turn heat to low. Season with salt and pepper. Serve hot.

Tortillitas

Shrimp Pancakes

These tasty thin pancakes are popular in the tapas bars of the Jerez region. Get ready to make two batches; they seem to get eaten very quickly!

Serves 6

1/2 cup chickpea flour

1/2 cup white flour

1/2 teaspoon baking powder

Salt and freshly ground black pepper

1 cup water

1/3 cup chopped onion or scallions

1/2 cup chopped raw shrimp

2 to 3 tablespoons chopped chives,
 parsley, thyme, or cilantro

Olive oil

Stir together the flours, baking powder, salt, and pepper. Add water and stir; mixture should resemble heavy cream. Stir in the onions, shrimp, and herbs. Heat enough olive oil to coat bottom of a nonstick pan; bring to high heat. Pour in half the batter, until it fills center of pan; spread gently with a spoon to form a large pancake. Cook about 3 minutes, or until pancake is set around the edges. Flip pancake and cook for 3 minutes; then flip it again and cook for another 30 seconds or so, until it is crisp on the outside but still moist inside. Remove from pan and serve first pancake immediately, while cooking remaining batter.

Canelones del Mare

Rolled Pasta with Scallop and Crab

This is the most popular dish at La Boca, my tapas restaurant in Santa Fe.

Serves 6

1 recipe Fresh Pasta (see page 140)

Seafood Cream Sauce

1 yellow onion, diced

2 tablespoons olive oil

1 tablespoon butter

2 quarts heavy cream, divided

1 cup white wine

2 tablespoons chopped sage

1 tablespoon chopped oregano

Salt and pepper to taste

2 cups shredded manchego cheese

2 pounds crabmeat

1 pound bay scallops

1/2 cup chopped parsley

1/2 cup bread crumbs

In a large pot, sauté onion in olive oil and butter until soft. Add cream and cook until mixture is reduced by about half. Add wine, herbs, and salt and pepper. Cook for 2 more minutes on medium-high heat. Remove from heat and stir in the cheese. Set aside to cool.

Combine crabmeat, scallops, parsley, 1 cup of the Seafood Cream Sauce, and bread crumbs.

> continued

Fresh Pasta

3 cups flour

4 whole eggs

1 tablespoon extra virgin olive oil

1 teaspoon salt

4 quarts water

Place the flour in a mound on a smooth, clean surface. Make a large well in the center of the mound with your fist. Pour the eggs into the well and beat them with a fork. Add the salt and olive oil to the egg mixture. Slowly start mixing the flour into the eggs by hand until all of the eggs and flour are mixed and a rough ball of dough is formed. Pick up the dough as well as you can and clean the work surface of any excess flour that would not mix in. Sprinkle a little fresh flour on the table and knead the dough for about 10 minutes. The ball of dough should be getting smoother now. Cover dough with a towel and let it rest at room temperature for about 30 minutes.

Cut the dough into 4 pieces. Working on a large cutting board, roll the dough very thin and cut it into 12 (4-by-5-inch) rectangles. Prepare a pot of boiling water (4 quarts) and boil the pasta rectangles for about 4 minutes; then transfer to a clean work surface. Dry the pasta with a towel.

Rolled Pasta

Heat the oven to 400 degrees. Place 3 tablespoons filling onto each pasta rectangle and roll up lengthwise. Place $1/2$ cup of Seafood Cream Sauce in the bottom of an ovenproof baking dish. Arrange the canelones on top of the sauce. Add the rest of the cream sauce evenly on top. Bake uncovered for 15–20 minutes, until the top is slightly browned and the filling is hot inside. Remove from oven and let rest for 5 minutes. Transfer canelones to serving plates with a spatula, 2 per person.

Pez Espada

Grilled Swordfish with Pomegranate

A few ingredients can make a very exotic dish. Good-quality fresh swordfish on the grill is always a crowd pleaser.

Serves 6

½ cup pomegranate molasses
4 cloves garlic, minced
¼ cup extra virgin olive oil
Juice of 1 lemon
2 crushed guindilla chiles or
  1 teaspoon red chile flakes
3 tablespoons chopped cilantro
6 (4-ounce) swordfish steaks,
  about 1 inch thick
Salt and pepper to taste

Whisk together all ingredients except fish and salt and pepper. Pour over fish as a marinade. Chill covered for 2 hours. Heat a grill to high heat. Season fish with salt and pepper. Grill steaks for about 4 minutes per side. Serve with a simple green salad.

Gambas Moros

Moroccan Grilled Shrimp

Spicy grilled shrimp are set off with a smooth, cooling sauce.

Serves 6

Shrimp

2 pounds shrimp

2 teaspoons ground cumin

2 teaspoons hot pimenton
  (Spanish paprika)

1 tablespoon crushed fennel seed

2 teaspoons cayenne pepper

1 tablespoon ground coriander

3 tablespoons extra virgin olive oil

Avocado Dipping Sauce

2 ripe avocados

2 teaspoons ground cumin

1 tablespoon lemon juice

2 tablespoons olive oil

¼ cup chopped cilantro

2 teaspoons salt

For the shrimp: Toss above ingredients with shrimp and refrigerate for 2 hours.

For the avocado dipping sauce: Heat the grill to high and grill the shrimp for 2 minutes per side. Serve hot with avocado dipping sauce.

Puree all ingredients well in a blender.

Croquettas de Cangrejo y Manchego

Manchego Crab Croquettes

These will disappear before they cool down.

Serves 6

Crab Mixture

4 tablespoons butter

1/4 cup finely chopped celery

1/4 cup finely chopped onion

1 tablespoon finely chopped red bell pepper

1/2 small clove garlic, finely minced

12 ounces lump crabmeat

2 cups (8 ounces) manchego cheese

2 green onions, finely chopped

2 eggs, lightly beaten

3 tablespoons mayonnaise

1 teaspoon sherry vinegar

1 1/2 cups soft bread crumbs

1/4 teaspoon cayenne pepper

4 tablespoons olive oil for frying

Freshly ground black pepper to taste

In a sauté pan, melt the butter over medium heat. Add the celery, onion, bell peppers, and garlic. Cook until soft, 3-4 minutes. In a large bowl, mix the crabmeat, cheese, green onions, eggs, mayonnaise, vinegar, bread crumbs, and cayenne. Stir in the sautéed vegetables. Cover and refrigerate about 2 hours.

Aioli

2 cloves garlic

1/2 cup roasted red bell pepper,
    peeled and roughly chopped

1 teaspoon fresh lemon juice

1/2 cup fresh basil

1/3 cup mayonnaise

2 tablespoons olive oil

Salt to taste

While the crab mixture is chilling, make the aioli by combining the garlic, roasted red pepper, lemon juice, basil, mayonnaise, and olive oil in a food processor bowl with a metal blade. Process until finely chopped. Season with salt and pepper to taste.

To complete the recipe, remove the crab mixture from the refrigerator and form 6 round cakes, 3 x 1 inch thick. Heat 4 tablespoons olive oil in a large skillet over medium heat. Cook the crab cakes 3–4 minutes per side, until golden brown and thoroughly heated. Serve with the aioli.

Salmone Curado Oloroso

Cured Salmon

Enjoy this delicious cured fish as it is eaten in Southern Spain. Note that the fish must be prepared six days ahead. Try this with tuna as well. The curing pulls the moisture out so the finished product can be sliced thin, with the texture of ham. Simple curing is fun to do; once you get the technique down, you will want to do more. Serve the cured salmon on toasts with capers, aioli and pickled onions. A more deluxe version might include some brie or manchego cheese.

Serves 4

1/2 cup kosher salt

3/4 cup brown sugar

1/2 cup oloroso sherry

2 tablespoons smoked paprika

1 pound salmon fillet

Mix salt, sugar, sherry, and paprika in a bowl. Coat the fish on both sides with the mixture. Put fish in a perforated pan above another pan to catch the juices. Refrigerate for 6 days. Slice thinly and serve on top of bread as a tapa.

Vieras con Morcilla

Seared Sea Scallops with Morcilla and Passion Fruit Cream

The briny sea breeze flavor of the scallops combines well with the rich, meaty blood sausage. Tart passion fruit helps balance the dish.

Serves 4

1/2 cup passion fruit puree

1/4 cup heavy cream

2 tablespoons butter

8 sea scallops

3 tablespoons olive oil

Pinch of salt

8 slices morcilla (Spanish blood sausage)

In a small saucepan, boil the passion fruit with the cream for about 2 minutes. Turn off heat and whisk in the butter. Keep warm.

Toss scallops with oil and salt. In a hot cast-iron pan, sear the scallops for about 1 minute per side. In the same pan, sear the morcilla until slightly crispy on both sides. Place a slice of morcilla on each scallop. Put two scallops on each plate and finish with the passion fruit sauce. Delicious!

Mejillones con Romesco

Mussels Steamed in Romesco Fish Broth

Romesco is a versatile condiment made with almonds, garlic, and red peppers. This dish is very simple and shows the Spanish passion for the affinity of shellfish and almonds. Try drinking an amontillado sherry with this.

Serves 4–6

2 pounds mussels

2 cups fish stock

1 cup Romesco Sauce

Stir together and steam in covered sauté pan until mussels open.

Romesco Sauce

1 cup almonds

2 roasted and peeled red bell peppers

6 cooked cloves garlic

$1/2$ cup extra virgin olive oil

1 tablespoon sherry vinegar

Salt

Blend all ingredients together until smooth.

Coca de Boquerones

White Anchovy Flatbread with Roncal Cheese

Arugula, almonds, orange zest, and extra virgin olive oil top Spanish flatbread, like pizza.

Serves 8

1 recipe Flatbread

4 ounces marinated white
  anchovies from Spain or Italy

2 roasted red bell peppers,
  peeled, julienned

1/2 cup white raisins

1 to 2 tablespoons extra virgin olive
  oil plus more for drizzling

2 cups shaved Roncal cheese

1 1/2 to 2 cups chopped arugula

Zest of 1 large or 2 small oranges

1/2 cup crushed Marcona almonds

Sea salt to taste

Preheat oven to 400 degrees. Top flatbread dough with anchovies, peppers, raisins, and 1–2 tablespoons olive oil. Bake 15 minutes. Remove from oven and top with cheese. Return to oven for 5 more minutes. When golden brown, remove from oven and top with arugula, orange zest, almonds, and sea salt to taste. Cut crosswise into 8 slices. Serve warm with a drizzle of extra virgin olive oil.

Flatbread

2 teaspoons yeast

1 teaspoon sugar

1/2 cup warm water

1 tablespoon olive oil

1 tablespoon white wine

2 teaspoons salt

1 3/4 to 2 cups flour

In medium bowl, combine yeast, sugar, warm water; let stand 10 minutes. Stir in olive oil and wine. Stir in salt and enough flour to make a smooth dough. Knead until smooth. Place dough in bowl; cover and let rise in a warm place for about 1 hour; then knead.

If baking without a topping, preheat the oven to 400 degrees. Lightly oil a baking sheet. On a lightly floured surface, roll dough to an 18 x 6-inch oblong, about 1/4 inch thick. Transfer to a baking sheet and cook until golden, about 12–15 minutes.

Vieras con Mahon

Sea Scallops with Orange-Parsnip Puree and Mahon Cheese

This rich and creamy winter scallop dish is taken to another level with a finish of hazelnut butter.

Serves 8

Scallops

1/2 cup olive oil

1/4 cup fresh orange juice

1 crushed bay leaf

1/2 teaspoon ground coriander
   seed, toasted

1/2 teaspoon crushed sea salt

1/4 teaspoon cracked black pepper

16 large sea scallops

Orange-Parsnip Puree

1 pound parsnips, peeled, cut in 2-inch pieces

Zest and juice of 1 orange

1/4 pound (1 stick) butter

Salt and pepper to taste

Hazelnut Butter

1 cup toasted hazelnuts

2 tablespoons sugar

1 teaspoon salt

1 1/2 cups (6 ounces) shredded Mahon cheese

For the scallops: In a glass dish or plastic bag, mix the olive oil, orange juice, bay leaf, coriander, sea salt, and cracked pepper. Add the scallops and stir to coat. Cover and refrigerate 1 hour to marinate.

For the orange-parsnip puree: Cook the parsnips in boiling water until tender, 10–15 minutes; drain. While still hot, combine the parsnips with the orange zest and juice, butter, and salt and pepper to taste. Process in a food processor or blender until smooth. Keep warm.

For the hazelnut butter: In a food processor, combine the hazelnuts, sugar, and salt. Process until a very smooth paste forms (the mixture is quite thick).

Heat the oven broiler to high. Heat a large sauté pan on high heat. Drain then sear sea scallops, about 3 minutes per side. Cover with the cheese. Place the pan under the broiler until the cheese is bubbling, about 1 minute. Serve 2 scallops per plate, with parsnip puree and hazelnut butter.

Sardinas Asadas
Grilled Sardines with Grilled Lemon Vinaigrette

The skin will blister and crackle with aromas of sea salt and lemon. The oily flesh becomes warm and soft as it slides off the bone into your mouth, while the lines between the sacred and profane begin to blur.

Makes about 3/4 cup

Juice of 2 lemons

6 cloves fresh garlic, peeled and minced

1 tablespoon sea salt

1/4 cup chopped fresh parsley

1/2 cup Spanish extra virgin olive oil

12 fresh sardines, gutted with head on

Heat an outdoor grill to high heat. Toss all ingredients in a bowl with the sardines. Let marinate at room temperature for 30 minutes. Grill for about 4 minutes per side. Transfer to a platter and top with Grilled Lemon Vinaigrette. Serve with lots of cold beer and crusty bread.

Grilled Lemon Vinaigrette

4 lemons , cut in half

4 cloves garlic, minced

1/4 cup Spanish extra virgin olive oil

1 teaspoon sea salt

Grill the lemons cut side down for 2 minutes on high heat. Turn and grill for another 2 minutes. Remove from grill. Allow to cool to room temp. Squeeze all the juice from the grilled lemons into a small bowl. Whisk in all other ingredients. Pour the mixture over a platter of grilled sardines. Also tastes great on grilled shrimp, tuna, beef steak, and grilled vegetables.

Meat
Tapas

Serranitos

Pork, Jamón, and Green Pepper Toasts

A classic meaty pincho whose name comes from the unmistakable jamón serrano.

Serves 6

1 pork tenderloin, trimmed of
　fat and white tendons

Salt and pepper to taste

4 New Mexico green chiles or Anaheim chiles

12 ($\frac{1}{2}$-inch) slices baguette

$\frac{1}{2}$ cup extra virgin olive oil, divided

6 slices jamón serrano, cut in half

12 pieces pickled green chile,
　piparras, or pepperoncini

Preheat oven to 350 degrees. Season the pork tenderloin with salt and pepper. Roast in the oven for 20 minutes; remove to cool. Roast the green chiles in the oven until charred and blackened. Transfer to a small bowl and cover with plastic wrap to allow the chiles to sweat, for ease when peeling.

Heat $\frac{1}{4}$ cup oil in a skillet and toast the bread slices in it. Peel and seed the chiles; cut into $\frac{1}{2}$-inch strips. Slice the tenderloin into 12 thin slices. Top each piece of toast with a slice of tenderloin, then a half slice of jamón, next a few strips of roasted green chile, and finally a piece of pickled chile. Secure all with toothpicks. Make a platter of serranitos and drizzle with remaining olive oil. Share with friends!

Pinchos de Chorizo y Huevo de Codorniz

Chorizo Toasts with Fried Quail Eggs

Quail eggs are common in the pinchos bars in San Sebastian, where you might come across a platter of these tasty toasts.

Serves 6

$\frac{1}{2}$ cup extra virgin olive oil, divided

12 ($\frac{1}{2}$-inch) slices of baguette

24 thin slices chorizo

12 quail eggs

Salt

Heat $\frac{1}{4}$ cup olive oil in a skillet and toast the bread slices in it. In another pan, heat a few tablespoons olive oil and cook the chorizo slices for about $1\frac{1}{2}$ minutes on medium heat, just enough to warm up the chorizo, crisp the edges, and release some of the tasty paprika-colored oil.

Top each toast with 2 pieces of chorizo and reserve the red oil in the pan. Fry the quail eggs in remaining olive oil with a sprinkle of salt—about 1 minute on one side for sunny side up. Top each toast with a fried egg and then drizzle the platter with chorizo oil.

Rilletes de Cerdo

Chilled Cooked Pork in Pork Fat

In the southern sherry region of Sanlúcar de Barrameda, this dish, covered in congealed pork fat, is served cold and often eaten for breakfast.

Serves 8

2 cups olive oil, divided

1 yellow onion, diced

4 cloves garlic, minced

2 pounds pork shoulder cut
   into 1/2-inch cubes

1 tablespoon sherry vinegar

2 teaspoons salt

1 tablespoon pimenton

1 cup cornichons for serving

1/2 cup Dijon mustard for serving

Bread for serving

In a deep sauté pan, heat 1/4 cup olive oil and sauté the onions and garlic on medium heat for 10 minutes. Add the pork, vinegar, salt, and pimenton and cook for 15 minutes. Add the remaining olive oil and cook for another 10 minutes. Then turn the heat down to low and cook covered for 1 1/2 hours.

Divide the mixture into eight small bowls or cazuelas, making sure each dish has plenty of olive oil on top. Cover and chill the dishes for 4 hours. Serve cold with cornichons, mustard, and bread.

Buey con Caramelo

Grilled Beef with Smoked Sea Salt Caramel

This more modern-style sauce relies on a specialty item: smoked sea salt. This sauce gives more sex appeal to simple grilled steak, but it can also be poured over ice cream.

Serves 8 as a tapa

2 pounds flat iron steak or hanger steak

Salt and pepper

Prepare a grill on medium-high heat. Sprinkle the steak generously with salt and pepper. Grill for about 4 minutes per side. Pull from grill and allow meat to rest for 1 minute. Slice and serve with Smoked Sea Salt Caramel Sauce.

Smoked Sea Salt Caramel Sauce

1 cup brown sugar

1 stick butter

2 tablespoons heavy cream

1 tablespoon pimenton

1½ tablespoons smoked sea salt

Melt the sugar and butter together in a saucepan over medium heat. Stir in the cream and cook for another 2 minutes. Stir in the pimenton and sea salt. Remove from heat and serve warm over grilled steak.

Carne Crudo

Raw Beef with Preserved Lemons, Piquillos, and Garlic Aioli

Preserved lemons can be purchased in specialty food stores. They usually come from Morocco, Tunisia, or Sicily, where they are popular. They're easy to make but take two to three weeks to cure.

Serves 6

12 ounces beef sirloin

2 teaspoons smoked sea salt

1 cup Piquillo-Garlic Confit (see page 101)

2 Preserved Lemons (see facing page),
   cut into very thin strips

Garlic Aioli

1 egg

2 cloves garlic

1 tablespoon lemon juice

1 teaspoon salt

3/4 cup extra virgin olive oil

Few tablespoons water, optional

Slice the raw beef into 1/4-inch strips and lay out on a large chilled plate. Top with salt, Piquillo Garlic Confit and Preserved Lemons. Drizzle the plate with Garlic Aioli.

For the garlic aioli: Put the egg, garlic, lemon juice, and salt into a blender. Puree well. While the motor is still running, slowly pour the olive oil into the blender until a thick mayo sauce forms. Thin this sauce by blending in a few tablespoons of water, if desired.

Preserved Lemons

Southern Spain is heavily influenced by Arabic/Moorish culture. Many versions of preserved lemons are on the market in specialty stores. They are always better when you make them yourself. The lemons are packed in salt, and when they are ready to be used, you will scrape away and discard the flesh of the lemon. You are left with the pungent and perfumy lemon rind, which has concentrated lemon flavor. I like to call it "Lemon Squared."

6 lemons, halved

Juice from 2 lemons

6 cloves garlic, peeled

1 cinnamon stick

10 whole cloves

1 cup sea salt

Combine all ingredients well in a bowl. Transfer to a glass jar with a tight-fitting lid. Keep the jar in a cool, dry place for 14–20 days. Remove the amount you want from the salt brine and rinse with cold water as needed. The remaining lemons can stay packed in salt another 3–4 weeks. When using, scrape the fleshy pulp from the skin and discard the pulp. Chop the preserved lemon rind very finely to use in recipes. Just a little is packed with big lemon flavor.

Pinchos de Pollo

Grilled Chicken Skewers with Harissa Couscous

The cooking of Southern Spain has strong Arabic roots, and the harissa shows off the spicy and aromatic North African flavors. The harissa chiles used in this region have a flavor similar to dried New Mexico red chiles.

Serves 6

6 boneless chicken thighs,
   cut into 1-inch cubes

2 tablespoons lemon juice

¼ cup olive oil

4 cloves garlic, minced

1 teaspoon ground cumin

1 tablespoon ground coriander

1 tablespoon dry oregano

1 teaspoon turmeric

Toss the chicken with all the other ingredients and let marinate in the refrigerator for 4 hours (up to 24 hours is ideal). Thread chicken evenly onto 6 wooden or metal skewers. Prepare a grill on medium-high heat and grill the skewers for about 5 minutes per side, until chicken is cooked through.

Harissa Couscous

2 cups dry couscous

2 cups chicken stock

2 tablespoons Harissa (see page 54)

Put the couscous in a large bowl. Heat the chicken stock and bring to a boil. Stir the Harissa into the chicken stock. Pour the hot stock over the couscous and cover with plastic wrap. Let stand for 15 minutes.

Divide harissa couscous onto 6 small plates and top each serving with a chicken skewer.

Cantimpalitos

Grilled Mini Chorizos with Potato Puree

Cantimpalitos are small, tasty chorizos made for the grill, flavored with paprika and garlic.

Serves 6

2 pounds potatoes, cut into quarters

¼ cup olive oil

6 cloves garlic

2 tablespoons butter

3 tablespoons heavy cream

1 tablespoon chopped fresh sage

Salt to taste

36 cantimpalitos (mini chorizos)

In a large pot of boiling water, boil the potatoes until soft. In a skillet, heat the olive oil and garlic together on medium heat for 7 minutes, until garlic is cooked through, soft, and brown. Drain the potatoes and put them in a food processor with the garlic, olive oil, butter, cream, sage, and salt. Puree well and set aside; keep hot.

Heat a grill to medium-high heat. Thread cantimpalitos onto skewers, 6 pieces per serving. Grill for 4 minutes per side. Divide potatoes onto 6 plates and top each serving with a skewer of grilled sausages.

Morcilla con Manzanas
Blood Sausage with Apples

The rich blood sausage is not overpowering and blends well in this classic European apple-sausage snack.

Serves 4

2 tablespooons olive oil

1 yellow onion, diced

2 golden delicious apples, diced with peel on

1 tablespoon chopped sage

Salt and pepper to taste

2 tablespoons white wine or oloroso sherry

2 links Morcilla blood sausage,
   cut into 12 slices

Olive oil

Heat the olive oil in a sauté pan over medium heat, and sauté the onions and apples with sage, salt, and pepper. Cook for 8 minutes. Add sherry and cook for 2 more minutes. Cook sliced morcilla on a *plancha* or cast-iron skillet lightly rubbed with olive oil. Cook slices on high heat for about 2 minutes per side, until morcilla is slightly crispy on the outside. Serve on top of apple mixture.

Patatas al Ajillo con Chorizo
Potatoes with Chorizo

Chorizo makes this rich potato dish slightly smoky and meaty.

Serves 4–6

2 pounds potatoes, sliced, not peeled

4 cups olive oil

16 cloves garlic, sliced

1 red bell pepper, diced

$1/2$ pound chopped chorizo

2 cups diced tomatoes

$1/4$ cup sherry vinegar

Salt and pepper to taste

$1/2$ cup chopped parsley

In saucepan, cover potatoes with olive oil and cook on medium heat until soft. Drain, reserving the oil.

In large sauté pan, cook the garlic and pepper in 2 cups of reserved oil until soft. Add chorizo and cook for 2 minutes. Add tomatoes, vinegar, cooked potatoes, and salt and pepper. Cook on low for 15 minutes. Toss with parsley.

Morcilla con Setas

Blood Sausage with Mushrooms, Spring Peas, and Mint Oil

The more I cook with Spanish morcilla, the more I am amazed at its versatility and its affection for many different flavors.

Serves 4

1 pound morcilla blood sausage

1 pound mushrooms, sliced

2 tablespoons olive oil

4 cloves garlic, slivered

Salt and pepper to taste

2 tablespoons white wine

1 cup shelled spring peas

1 tablespoon chopped fresh mint

2 tablespoons mint oil

Mint Oil

½ cup extra virgin olive oil

½ cup chopped mint

Pinch of salt

Cut the blood sausage into 12 slices. Sauté the mushrooms in olive oil with garlic, salt, and pepper for 5 minutes. Add the wine and cook for 2 more minutes. Boil the peas for 2 minutes and drain. When mushrooms are done, remove from heat and stir in the peas.

In a cast-iron skillet, sear the morcilla in a dry pan for 2 minutes per side. Arrange the slices of morcilla down the middle of a platter. Surround with mushroom/pea mixture and drizzle the plate with the mint oil.

For the mint oil: In a small saucepan over medium heat, heat olive oil to warm. Remove from heat and add the mint and a small pinch of salt. Allow to rest for 1 hour. Drain through a sieve. Reserve extra mint oil for other uses, such as a vinaigrette.

Kefta

Grilled Ground Lamb

After cooking these Moroccan-style hand-formed sausages on the grill, try them in a little sandwich or wrapped in Yogurt Flatbread (see page 104).

Serves 6

2 pounds ground lamb

1 yellow onion, minced

1 tablespoon ground cumin

1 teaspoon ground cinnamon

2 tablespoons chopped fresh cilantro

3 cloves garlic, minced

2 tablespoons chopped fresh mint

1 tablespoon pimenton

2 eggs

2 cups bread crumbs

Salt and pepper to taste

Yogurt for serving

Tomatoes for serving

Mix all ingredients together in a bowl with a wooden spoon. Refrigerate for 1 hour. Form into 2- inch-long football shapes. Prepare a grill on medium-high heat. Grill sausages for about 3 minutes per side. Serve with yogurt and tomatoes.

Canelones de Morcilla

Blood Sausage-and-Beet Canelones

This dish offers a balance of rich and meaty flavors along earthy beets and beet greens. The canelones are baked in a Roasted Red Pepper Cream Sauce.

Serves 6

1 pound beets

1 yellow onion, diced

¼ cup Spanish olive oil

3 cloves garlic, minced

1 pound morcilla blood sausage, diced

3 cups chopped beet greens

Salt and pepper to taste

1 recipe Fresh Pasta (see page 140)

Roasted Red Pepper Cream (see facing page)

Heat the oven to 375 degrees. Clean the beets and roast in the oven until a sharp knife will readily pierce through to the center of the beets. When cool enough to handle, slip off the skins and dice.

Sauté onion in olive oil. Add garlic. Add cooked beets and morcilla; stir. Cook for 1 more minute. Stir in the beet greens. Remove from heat. Add salt and pepper to taste.

Roll out and cut pasta dough into rectangles according to the recipe on page 140.

Place 4 tablespoons filling on each pasta rectangle and roll to close. Spread ½ cup Roasted Red Pepper Cream in the bottom of an ovenproof baking dish. Arrange the canelones on the sauce. Top with the remaining sauce and bake uncovered for 20 minutes.

Roasted Red Pepper Cream

1 yellow onion, diced

¼ cup olive oil

2 tablespoons butter

2 quarts heavy cream

1 cup white wine

2 tablespoons chopped fresh parsley

1 tablespoon chopped fresh oregano

Salt and pepper to taste

2 roasted red bell peppers, peeled, seeded, and diced

Sauté onion in olive oil and butter until soft. Add heavy cream and reduce by about half. Add wine, herbs, and salt and pepper. Add the roasted red peppers and cook for 2 more minutes on medium-high heat. Remove from heat and set aside to cool.

Corazon

Grilled Beef Heart with Romesco

Heart is an uncommon meat, but when you find it, give it a try. On the grill it is tender and has more flavor than many other cuts.

Serves 6

1 large beef heart, excess fat removed

6 cloves garlic, slivered

¼ cup sherry vinegar

½ cup olive oil

1 tablespoon ground cumin

Salt to taste

Romesco Sauce (see page 149)

Cut heart into four pieces. Mix garlic, vinegar, olive oil, and cumin for a marinade. Pour over heart pieces and marinate in the refrigerator for at least 1 hour.

Heat a grill to medium-high heat. Slice heart into ¼-inch slices and grill, adding a sprinkle of salt. Grill for 2 minutes per side. Serve hot off the grill with warm bread and Romesco Sauce.

Pollo con Pedro Ximenez

PX Chicken with Garlic and Oranges

PX is shorthand for Pedro Ximenez, a rich and syrupy sweet, figgy sherry. The oranges provide a nice balance. This dish has a deep, exotic Andalucian flavor. Your chicken will thank you!

Serves 6

¼ cup olive oil

15 whole cloves garlic

½ yellow onion, finely diced

6 boneless chicken thighs

1 teaspoon salt

½ teaspoon pepper

1 teaspoon sherry vinegar

¼ cup orange juice

½ cup chicken stock

½ cup Pedro Ximenez sherry

3 oranges, peeled and divided into segments

In a large skillet, heat the olive oil over high heat. Add the garlic and cook for 7 minutes. Add the onion and cook until soft. Add the chicken and sprinkle with salt and pepper. After 5 minutes, turn the chicken over and cook for another 3 minutes. Turn heat down to medium. Remove chicken from the pan and set aside. Add the vinegar, orange juice, chicken stock, and sherry to the pan and whisk well. Cook and reduce for 3 minutes. Add chicken back to the pan and cook uncovered until chicken is cooked through. Turn off heat and toss orange segments into the pan with the other ingredients. Divide chicken onto six small plates and cover with sauce.

Higado de Pato

Foie Gras with PX Glaze and Grilled Pineapple

The Pedro Ximenez sherry likes foie gras as much as it likes ice cream. The pineapple adds some punchy bright notes of counterpoint to the dark, rich dish.

Serves 6

6 (½-inch) slices fresh pineapple

2 tablespoons turbinado sugar

Salt and pepper to taste, divided

12 ounces foie gras, cut into
  6 (2-ounce) pieces

½ cup Pedro Ximenez sherry

½ cup chicken stock

Heat a gas grill to high heat. Sprinkle the pineapple with sugar, salt, and pepper. Grill for 3 minutes per side then set aside.

Heat a large skillet to high heat. Sprinkle the foie gras slices with salt and pepper on both sides. Place the foie gras in the hot dry pan. Sear for 2 minutes per side. Remove from pan and set aside. Turn heat down to medium. Whisk in the sherry and chicken stock. Cook and reduce for about 4 minutes, until the mixture becomes syrupy.

Divide pineapple pieces among 6 small plates. Add the foie gras back to the pan with the sauce and heat for 1 minute. Top each pineapple piece with a piece of seared foie gras and top each plate with a few tablespoons of sauce.

Pato con Idiazabal

Pan-Seared Duck Breast with Melted Idiazabal, Mango, and Smoky Cashew Butter

This is a more modern-style tapa with layering of flavors and textures. The Basque cheese Idiazabal makes any dish more interesting, but when paired with mango, duck, and cashew this tapa becomes an exotic mini feast.

Serves 4

1 tablespoon ground coriander

1 teaspoon ground cumin

1 teaspoon ground anise seed

1 tablespoon honey

2 cloves garlic, minced

2 teaspoons salt

1 teaspoon black pepper

1 tablespoon sherry vinegar

2 tablespoons olive oil

2 small duck breasts

Combine all ingredients with the duck in a bowl and marinate overnight.

Heat a sauté pan to high heat and sear the duck breasts, skin side first, for 1 minute. Turn heat down to medium and cook for another 3 minutes. Turn the breasts over and cook for 3 more minutes. Turn off heat. Allow duck to rest.

To Plate

1 ripe mango
4 ounces Idiazabal cheese
Smoky Cashew Butter

Heat oven to 350 degrees. Peel and cut mango into 8 wedges. Cut cheese into 8 slices. Cut each duck breast into 4 slices. Arrange the 8 slices of duck breast on a sheet pan. Top each with a piece of mango and a slice of cheese. Bake for 5 minutes. Serve 2 duck breast slices per plate with 1 tablespoon of Smoky Cashew Butter next to the duck.

Smoky Cashew Butter

Makes about 1 cup

1 cup roasted cashews (unsalted)
¼ cup extra virgin olive oil
2 teaspoons smoked sea salt
2 teaspoons pimenton

Blend well in food processor. Serve at room temperature.

Garbanzos con Chicharrónes

Chickpeas with Lamb Chicharrónes

When you trim lamb to make lamb chops, you will end up with lots of fat. Here is a great use for some of it. The chicharrónes are fried skin with fat attached.

Serves 6

1/4 cup plus 2 tablespoons
   extra virgin olive oil

2 cups lamb fat, cut into 1/2-inch cubes

Salt to taste

1 yellow onion, diced

1 teaspoon ground cumin seed

4 cups cooked garbanzo beans

1 tablespoon chopped cilantro

1 tablespoon chopped mint

2 tablespoons Sofrito (see page 74)

1/4 cup oloroso sherry

Heat 1/4 cup olive oil in a small sauté pan and cook the lamb fat on high heat for 20 minutes. Remove chicharrónes from the oil and lay them on paper towels. Sprinkle with a little salt. Set aside to cool.

In a large sauté pan, sauté the onion in 2 tablespoons olive oil until soft. Add all other ingredients, including the chicharrónes, and simmer for 7 minutes. Serve in 6 small bowls with bread.

Pato en Vinegretta

Roasted Duck Breast with Blood Orange Vinaigrette and Olives

Rich duck breast meat always cries out for some citrus for balance. This recipe can be served hot or cold and would go nicely with a Mediterranean salad of dried apricots and figs (see page 43).

Serves 4

2 duck breasts, fat on

1 tablespoon chopped fresh rosemary

1 teaspoon sea salt

1 onion, finely chopped

1 clove garlic, minced

4 tablespoons chopped pitted
   Manzanilla olives

Rinse the duck breasts and pat dry with paper towels. With fat side lying up, cut through the fat in gashes about 1 inch apart. Season breasts with the rosemary and salt, making sure some rosemary gets into the cuts. Fry duck breasts in a nonstick, heavy-bottomed pan for about 2–3 minutes on each side, until meat is browned and fat is starting to get crispy. Remove from heat and cool until duck can be handled. Slice the breast into 1/2-inch-thick slices. They should still be quite raw in the middle.

In the duck fat left in the pan, fry the onion and garlic until caramelized. Add duck breast and olives and cook until meat is cooked, about 5 minutes. Remove from heat and lay the duck out on a platter. Top with Blood Orange Vinaigrette and olives.

Blood Orange Vinaigrette

Makes 1/2 cup

Juice of 2 blood oranges

1 tablespoon honey

1/4 cup olive oil

1 tablespoon sherry vinegar

1 teaspoon salt

1 teaspoon pepper

Whisk all ingredients together.

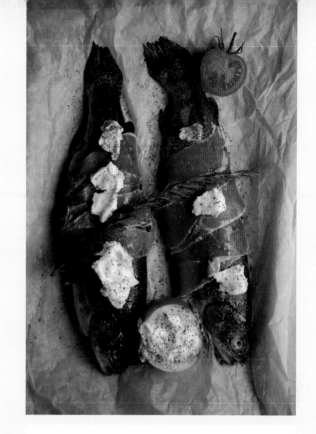

Main Dishes

Caballa al Horno

Whole Roasted Mackerel with Pipérade Puree

Pipérade is a classic Basque sweet red pepper stew that is enjoyed on top of omelets, with grilled fish or on its own. In this dish, the stew is pureed to become the perfect sauce for the big flavors of the mackerel. Really delicious served with sautéed spinach.

Serves 6

Pipérade puree
1/4 cup olive oil
2 guindilla chiles, crushed
8 cloves garlic, peeled
1/4 cup white wine
2 whole Spanish mackerel
Salt
Juice of 1 lemon
1/4 cup chopped parsley

Heat oven to 350 degrees. Prepare the Pipérade and puree it. Put in a small saucepan and set aside. In a large skillet, heat the olive oil on high heat. Add the chiles, garlic, and wine. Add the mackerel and cook for about 2 minutes per side. Transfer to a baking dish and pour the oil, garlic, and wine mixture over the fish. Sprinkle fish with salt. Add the lemon juice and parsley and bake uncovered for 20 minutes. Remove from the oven and allow to rest for 5 minutes. Heat the Pipérade sauce. Remove fillets from the bone and divide the meat onto 6 plates. Cover each portion with 3–4 tablespoons of sauce.

Pipérade Puree

Makes about 2 1/2 cups

1/4 cup Spanish extra virgin olive oil
1 yellow onion, peeled and julienned
2 red bell peppers, julienned
1 green bell pepper, julienned
2 tablespoons Spanish sherry vinegar
1 tablespoon hot pimenton
1/4 cup oloroso sherry
2 tablespoons chopped Italian parsley

Heat the oil in a 12-inch sauté pan on medium heat. Add the onions and sauté until transparent. Add the peppers and cook until they're soft, about 3–4 minutes. Add vinegar to the mixture and stir well. Add pimenton and sherry. Turn the heat down to low and cook for 45 minutes. This long, slow cooking will really coax out the natural sweetness of the peppers and onions. Stir in the parsley, remove from heat, and cool. Puree well.

Lacon de Puerco

Slow Braised Pork Shoulder with Mushrooms, Shallots, and Herbs

The braising method of low and slow cooking transforms tough cuts into meltingly tender hunks of meat that can barely keep their shape.

Serves 6

4-pound pork shoulder roast

Salt and pepper

½ cup plus 2 tablespoons olive oil, divided

2 onions, diced

2 carrots, diced

6 cloves garlic, peeled

6 whole shallots, peeled

3 cups red wine

2 bay leaves

Water

3 cups mushrooms, sliced

2 tablespoons chopped sage

2 tablespoons thyme leaves

Rub the roast with salt and pepper. Heat ¼ cup olive oil in a large skillet over high heat. Brown the meat on all sides. Remove meat from pan. Add ¼ cup more olive oil and the onions, carrots, garlic, and whole shallots. Cook for about 15 minutes on medium heat. Add the wine and stir to loosen any flavor bits stuck to the pan.

Preheat the oven to 300 degrees. Put the roast in a deep pan and pour the sautéed vegetables over the roast. Add the bay leaves and enough water to cover the roast. Cover the pan with a lid or foil. Cook in the oven for 4 hours. Remove from the oven. Remove roast from pan and reserve juices.

Sauté the mushrooms in a separate pan with 2 tablespoons olive oil, sage, and thyme. Pour the cooking liquid from the roast over the sautéed mushrooms. Cut the roast into 6 thick slices and arrange them on a serving platter. Top with the mushroom sauce.

Chuletas de Cordero con Salsa Agridulce
Grilled Lamb Chops with Chile-Mint Sauce

Simply grilled lamb chops are livened up here with a modern sauce that uses ancient flavors of honey, lemon, garlic, and mint.

Serves 4–6

4–6 lamb chops

Olive oil

Coarse salt and freshly ground black pepper

Chile-Mint Sauce

Preheat a charcoal or gas grill to medium-high. Grill the lamb chops for about 5 minutes per side, or until cooked: 130 degrees internal temperature for rare; 140 degrees for medium rare. (Use a thermometer to be sure.)

Chile-Mint Sauce

You can use this sweet-and-sour sauce on any kind of grilled meat, even tuna or swordfish.

Makes 1 cup

$1/2$ cup lemon juice

$1/2$ cup honey

$1/4$ cup chopped mint

3 tablespoons crushed red pepper flakes

1 teaspoon minced garlic

In a small bowl combine all ingredients.

Arroz con Calamares
Rice with Squid

A short-grain rice like the calasparra and bomba varieties are perfect for the endless Spanish dishes that use seafood. The rice absorbs flavors very well and has the perfect amount of starch.

Serves 4

¼ cup Spanish extra virgin olive oil

2 onions, diced

6 cloves garlic, slivered

1 red bell pepper, diced

2 tomatoes, diced

2 pounds fresh squid, cleaned
   and cut into ½-inch rings

2 cups calasparra rice

Juice of 1 lemon

1 cup white wine

⅓ cup chopped parsley

4½ cups fish stock

2 dried guindilla chiles, crushed, or
   1 teaspoon crushed chile flakes

In a large sauté pan or paella pan, heat the olive oil on high heat. Sauté the onions, garlic, bell pepper, and tomatoes for about 15 minutes. Add the squid and sauté for 4 minutes more. Turn the heat down to medium; add the rice and stir for about 2 minutes. Add remaining ingredients. Bring the mixture to a boil and then turn it down to low heat for about 15 minutes, until the rice grains are soft. Serve from the pan.

Cana de Cordero

Slow-Braised Lamb Shanks with Lemon, Cumin, and Cinnamon

This dish has a Moroccan flavor profile, and these shanks will fall off the bone.

Serves 4

4 whole lamb shanks

Salt and pepper

1/2 cup olive oil, divided

2 onions, diced

2 tomatoes, diced

2 carrots, diced

6 cloves garlic, peeled

2 stalks of celery, diced

3 cups red wine

2 lemons, quartered

2 tablespoons cumin seed, toasted

1 teaspoon ground cinnamon

Cooked rice or couscous

Heat the oven to 300 degrees. Rub the shanks with salt and pepper. Heat a large skillet to high heat with 1/4 cup olive oil. Brown the meat on all sides. Remove meat from pan. Add 1/4 cup more olive oil and the onions, tomatoes, carrots, garlic, and celery. Cook for about 15 minutes on medium heat. Add the wine and stir to loosen any flavor bits stuck to the pan. Add the lemons, cumin, and cinnamon, and cook for 5 minutes more.

Put the shanks in a large ovenproof pan and cover with the vegetable-wine mixture. Add enough water to cover the shanks in liquid. Cook covered for 5 hours. Transfer to a serving platter and serve with rice or couscous.

Matambre de Cerdo

Stuffed Pork Tenderloin

This pork tenderloin is stuffed with mushrooms and jamón serrano.

Serves 4

2 pork tenderloins, trimmed of fat

Salt and pepper

$1/2$ cup extra virgin olive oil

1 yellow onion, diced

4 cloves garlic, slivered

$1/2$ cup finely diced jamón serrano

4 cups diced mushrooms

2 tablespoons chopped parsley

1 tablespoon chopped sage

$1/2$ cup Spanish white wine

Heat the oven to 350 degrees. Open the tenderloins with a full-length cut that goes about $3/4$ of the way through the meat. Flatten out the tenderloin and season it on both sides with salt and pepper. Set aside.

Heat the olive oil in a skillet, and sauté the onion and garlic on medium heat for 12 minutes. Add the jamón, mushrooms, parsley, and sage; continue cooking for 20 minutes. Add the wine and cook for 5 more minutes. Remove from heat and allow to cool. Spread the mixture over the flattened tenderloin. Roll tenderloin around the filling and set it on a sheet pan with the seam side down. Roast in the oven for 25 minutes. Remove from oven and cut into 1-inch slices. Serve 2 slices per plate.

Lengua

Braised Beef Tongue with Carrot Puree and Fruit Relish

Beef tongue is an underrated and underused cut of meat. Long, slow braising will bring out a rich sweetness. This dish would fit right next to the turkey for a holiday buffet.

Serves 4

2 whole beef tongues

½ yellow onion, diced

½ cup diced celery

½ cup diced carrot

4 cloves garlic, crushed

4 cups beef stock

2 cups red wine (Tempranillo)

¼ cup olive oil

1 teaspoon ground black pepper

1 teaspoon ground cinnamon

2 teaspoons salt

To Plate

2 teaspoons olive oil

Salt to taste

Roasted Carrot Puree (recipe facing)

Fruit Relish (recipe facing)

Put all ingredients in a large saucepan and bring to a boil. Turn down to low heat and cover. Let simmer for 4 hours, until tongue is tender. Allow to cool in liquid. Peel the skin from the tongue.

To plate: Heat a plancha or cast-iron pan to high heat. Cut the tongue into 8 pieces. Drizzle the tongue slices with olive oil and a sprinkling of salt. Cook on plancha for 40 seconds per side, until surface of meat is slightly crispy. Put 2 tablespoons of warm carrot puree on each plate and top with 2 slices of tongue. Put a tablespoon of room-temperature Fruit Relish on each plate next the carrot puree.

Roasted Carrot Puree

Makes 4 cups

1 pound carrots, peeled and
 cut into 3-inch pieces
$^1/_4$ yellow onion, chopped
4 cloves garlic
3 tablespoons olive oil
$^1/_2$ teaspoon salt
2 tablespoons butter

Heat oven to 350 degrees. In a bowl, toss together all the ingredients except the butter. Spread on a sheet pan, and roast covered until cooked through, about 40 minutes. Remove from oven and puree well in a food processor, along with the butter. Serve hot.

Fruit Relish

Makes 1 $^1/_4$ cups

1 cup red grapes
3 tablespoons extra virgin olive oil, divided
1 teaspoon salt
$^1/_2$ teaspoon black pepper
$^1/_2$ yellow onion, diced
1 cup red wine
1 tablespoon red wine vinegar
$^1/_2$ cup chopped dried black figs
2 tablespoons whole grain Dijon mustard
$^1/_4$ cup brown sugar
Zest of $^1/_2$ lime
1 teaspoon red chile flakes
$^1/_2$ teaspoon ground star anise
3 tablespoons chopped bitter chocolate

Heat oven to 350 degrees. Toss the grapes with 1 tablespoon olive oil and salt and pepper. Roast grapes in the oven for 10 minutes. Remove from oven. Sauté the onion in 2 tablespoons olive oil on medium heat for 10 minutes. Add wine and vinegar, and cook until liquid reduces by half. Add the roasted grapes and all remaining ingredients; simmer for 15 minutes. Cool to room temperature.

Paella de Gambas y Chorizo
Shrimp and Chorizo Paella

There are as many versions of paella in Spain as there are cooks. You can add your own touches to this basic recipe by adding chicken, crab, duck, blood sausage, or green beans.

Serves 4

1 cup olive oil, divided

2 links dry chorizo, sliced

1 yellow onion, diced

1 tablespoon minced garlic

2 cups calasparra short-grain rice

2 cups Sofrito (see page 74)

2 tablespoons pimenton

2 pinches saffron

2½ cups fish stock or clam juice

2½ cups chicken stock

24 large raw shrimp, peeled

½ cup green peas

Sea salt and freshly ground black pepper

½ cup thin strips piquillo peppers

Make the paella on the stovetop in a large skillet or paella pan without a lid. In the pan, heat ¼ cup olive oil and cook the chorizo for about 3 minutes. Remove from pan and set aside. In the same pan, heat ¼ cup more olive oil and sauté onion until soft. Add garlic. Add rice and stir until each grain is coated with oil. Add the saffron.

Combine the fish stock or clam juice with chicken stock in a separate pan to make cooking liquid. Add 3 cups of the cooking liquid to the rice and bring to a simmer. Cook for about 5–7 minutes, until rice grains are soft. Add 3 cups of the cooking liquid to the rice, sofrito, pimenton, and saffron. Bring to a simmer and cook for about 5–7 minutes, until rice grains are soft. Add shrimp, peas, salt, and pepper; cook for 10 minutes. Then arrange the pequillo peppers on top.

Pato con Cus Cus

Couscous with Duck and Apricots

A nice southern-style combination of flavors: cumin, orange, and parsley.

Serves 6

2 whole duck legs

4 duck breasts, cut into 4 pieces

Salt and black pepper

1/2 cup olive oil, divided

2 yellow onions, diced

2 carrots, diced

4 cloves garlic, peeled and sliced

1 bunch green onions, chopped

2 cups chopped dried apricots

2 tablespoons chopped parsley

2 tablespoons ground cumin, toasted

1/2 cup red wine

3 cups chicken stock

1 cup orange juice

2 cups couscous

Heat the oven to 350 degrees. Season the duck with salt and pepper. Heat a large skillet with 1/4 cup olive oil. Brown the duck pieces on all sides and remove from pan. Add 1/4 cup more olive oil and sauté the onions, carrots, garlic, and green onions Add all remaining ingredients except couscous and bring to a boil. Pour the dry couscous into an ovenproof baking dish and arrange duck pieces on top of it. Pour the contents of the skillet over the duck and bake covered for 1 hour. Serve from the pan.

Salmon Picada

Almond-Crusted Salmon

The salmon is baked with a smooth crust of almonds, garlic, and bread.

Serves 6

Picada

2 cups extra virgin olive oil, divided

10 cloves garlic

6 (¹/₂-inch) baguette slices

2 cups Marcona almonds

1 cup chopped parsley

3 teaspoons salt

1 side salmon fillet

Mediterranean Salad (see page 43)

Heat the oven to 350 degrees. Heat 1 cup of olive oil in a skillet and add the garlic. Cook on medium heat for about 10 minutes, until garlic is soft and brown. Remove garlic with a slotted spoon and set aside. Toast the bread in the garlic-flavored oil for about 2 minutes per side. Set aside. Turn off heat and let everything cool. In a food processor, make picada by combining the almonds, toasted bread, remaining olive oil, and parsley. Add salt and puree well.

Place the salmon on a baking sheet, skin side down. Spread the Picada mixture evenly over the fillet. Cover with foil and bake for 15 minutes. Remove foil and bake for another 10 minutes. Serve with Mediterranean Salad.

Lomo de Cerdo con Gambas y Romesco

Pork Tenderloin with Grilled Shrimp and Romesco Sauce

There is a tasty tradition in Spain, called Mar y Montano, of mixing pork and other meats with seafood. The Romesco Sauce is rugged and refined enough to go with both pork and shrimp.

Serves 6

2 pork tenderloins, cleaned and trimmed,
   cut into 12 (½-inch) medallions

12 large shrimp, peeled and deveined

2 teaspoons salt

1 teaspoon ground pepper

¼ cup chopped parsley

½ cup Spanish extra virgin olive oil, divided

3 tablespoons lemon juice

Romesco Sauce (see page 149)

Heat a plancha or cast-iron skillet to medium-high heat. Season both the pork slices and the shrimp the same way: with salt, pepper, parsley, and ¼ cup of the olive oil, and lemon juice. Sear the pork first and cook for about 4 minutes per side. Transfer to a large platter. In the same pan, cook the shrimp in the remaining pork fat for about 2 minutes per side. Arrange the shrimp on top of the cooked pork slices. Spoon Romesco Sauce over the entire dish, drizzle with remaining olive oil, and serve as a shared tapa.

Bonito con Salsa Piquillo

Grilled Tuna in Piquillo Brandy Cream

A simple sauce of heavy cream and piquillo peppers makes this Basque-style dish hard to resist.

Serves 6

$^1/_2$ cup olive oil, divided

1 tablespoon butter

1 yellow onion, diced

4 whole shallots, peeled

6 piquillo peppers

4 cloves garlic, slivered

Salt

$^1/_2$ cup Spanish brandy

$^1/_2$ cup heavy cream

6 (6-ounce) fresh tuna steaks

Black pepper

$^1/_4$ cup chopped parsley

1 tablespoon lemon juice

6 cups salad greens, lightly dressed

Heat a sauté pan to high heat with $^1/_4$ cup olive oil and the butter. Add the onion and shallots and cook until soft. Add the piquillos, garlic, and a pinch of salt. After 4 minutes, turn the piquillos over and brown the other side. Add the brandy and cook for 2 more minutes. Remove from heat and puree well with the cream. Set aside in a small saucepan.

Heat a sauté pan to high heat with $^1/_4$ cup olive oil. Season the fish with salt, pepper, parsley, and lemon juice. Sear in the pan for 2 minutes per side for rare steaks. Set steaks on a serving platter; warm the sauce and pour over the tuna. Serve with a lightly dressed salad.

Chuletas de Cordero con Melocotones

Sage and Canela-Rubbed Lamb Chops with Grilled Peaches

Wait until peaches are in season and grill them lightly with a crumble of blue cheese for a unique late-summer side dish.

Serves 8

2 tablespoons chopped fresh sage

6 cloves garlic, minced

1 tablespoon ground cinnamon,
  preferably canela

2 teaspoons kosher salt

1/2 cup olive oil

16 thick-cut lamb chops

4 cups Spanish Tempranillo wine
  or Cabernet Sauvignon

1 cup beef or veal stock

2 tablespoons butter

4 ripe peaches

1 cup crumbled Cabrales blue cheese

In small bowl, make a paste of the sage, garlic, cinnamon, salt, and olive oil. Rub onto lamb. Marinate in refrigerator for 1 to 2 hours.

Combine the wine and stock in a large saucepan. Bring to a boil over medium heat. Simmer about 30 to 40 minutes, until reduced to about 1$1/2$ cups. Turn heat to low and stir in butter. Set aside and keep warm.

Heat a charcoal or gas grill to medium-high. Grill the lamb chops 4 minutes per side. Cut peaches in half and remove pits. Grill 1 minute on each side. Arrange lamb and peaches on a platter. Drizzle with wine sauce. Sprinkle blue cheese over the top just before serving.

Pollo Harissa

Roasted Harissa Chicken with Couscous

This whole chicken will be aromatic with a fiery, spicy skin and moist lemony meat inside. Try this with some Yogurt Flatbread (see page 104).

Serves 4

1 whole roasting chicken, rinsed

1 lemon, cut into 4 pieces

6 cloves garlic

Harissa (see page 54)

Salt

2 cups couscous

3 cups chicken stock

Heat the oven to 375 degrees. Fill chicken cavity with lemon pieces and garlic. Rub the chicken generously with harissa. Sprinkle with salt. Put the couscous and chicken stock in an oven-safe baking dish. Place the dressed chicken on top. Bake covered for 45 minutes. Remove the cover and bake for another 15 minutes, until chicken is cooked through. Serve with a tossed mix of cucumber, cilantro, lemon juice, and oil.

Truchas con Jamón

Baked Trout with Jamón Serrano and Rosemary

Roasting the whole fish with head and bones and all will bring out the rich, nutty flavor of the trout.

Serves 4

4 rainbow trout, gutted and
 left whole with head on

Salt and black pepper to taste

2 cloves garlic, minced

2 tablespoons lemon juice

2 tablespoons chopped parsley

8 slices jamón serrano

4 whole sprigs rosemary

¼ cup Spanish extra virgin olive oil

3 tablespoons butter

Preheat oven to 450 degrees. Season the fish inside and out with salt, pepper, garlic, lemon juice, and parsley. Wrap each trout with 2 slices of jamón. Top each trout with a sprig of rosemary. Put the fish on a baking sheet or in a ceramic dish. Pour olive oil over the fish. Break up the butter into pieces and put the pieces on top of the trout. Bake for 30 minutes, until jamón is crispy and the fish is cooked through. Serve with sautéed vegetables.

Desserts

Fresas

Strawberries in Pedro Ximenez Sweet Vinegar

Strawberries are harvested in abundance in Spain, and this dessert celebrates the juicy red gems. Pedro Ximenez is a rich, syrupy sweet sherry that is balanced with sherry vinegar to dress the fruit. Serve with whipped cream or a custardy crème anglaise.

Serves 6

1/2 cup Pedro Ximenez sherry

1/4 cup sherry vinegar

1/4 cup sugar

2 pounds strawberries

Zest of 1 orange

Cook sherry, vinegar, and sugar together on medium heat for
10 minutes. Let cool then toss with berries and zest. Serve with cream.

Crema Catalana

Cardamom Saffron Custard

This rich, creamy dessert is much more flavorful than its better-known relative crème brûlée.

Serves 4

2 cups whole milk, divided

1 pinch saffron threads

¼ teaspoon ground cardamom

3 egg yolks

1 cup powdered sugar

2½ tablespoons cornstarch

4 teaspoons granulated sugar

In a saucepan, combine 1½ cups of the milk with the saffron threads and cardamom. Bring the mixture to a boil then remove from the heat. Using a mixer, beat together the egg yolks and powdered sugar until the mixture is fluffy and light in color. With the mixer running, slowly pour the hot milk into the egg yolk mixture. Pour the mixture back into the saucepan.

In a small bowl, stir together the cornstarch and remaining ½ cup milk. Add this to the saucepan and turn the heat to medium. Cook, stirring, until the mixture thickens enough to coat the back of a wooden spoon. Pour the hot mixture into 4 ramekins and sprinkle the top of each custard with 1 teaspoon sugar. Arrange the ramekins on a cookie sheet and place it under a hot broiler just long enough for the sugar to caramelize. (If you have a propane torch you can use it to caramelize the sugar instead.) Serve immediately.

Trufas Carajillo

Espresso–Spanish Brandy Truffles

These truffles are named after the beverage carajillo, which is espresso with Spanish brandy, enjoyed in the afternoon.

Serves 6

2 cups chopped milk chocolate

2 tablespoons butter

2 cups heavy cream

1/2 cup powdered sugar

3 tablespoons good Spanish brandy

1 shot strong espresso

1/2 cup cocoa powder

Chop the chocolate into small pieces. Melt in a double boiler and add the butter and cream; mix well with a whisk. Add the powdered sugar, brandy, and espresso. Continue stirring well to form a thick mixture. Chill for 30 minutes. Roll into small balls. Dust generously with cocoa powder. Serve on a chilled platter.

Pestinos

Fried Orange-Anise Pastries

The Moorish influences of orange, honey, and sesame sing out in this Andalucian holiday cookie.

Makes 16

4³/₄ cups olive oil, divided

Zest of 2 oranges

1 tablespoon sesame seeds plus
   more for sprinkling

1 tablespoon anise seeds

¹/₄ cup oloroso sherry

2 tablespoons butter

1 tablespoon vegetable
   shortening or pork fat

¹/₂ teaspoon ground cinnamon

Zest of 1 lemon

1 teaspoon salt

2¹/₄ cups flour, plus extra for dusting

Orange Glaze (recipe follows)

Orange Glaze

2 tablespoons orange juice

¹/₂ cup water

¹/₂ cup honey

Add ³/₄ cup olive oil to a small sauté pan along with the orange zest. Heat on medium for about 2 minutes. Remove from heat and allow to cool to room temperature. Strain and discard the zest, reserving the orange-flavored oil. Add sesame seeds and anise seeds to the oil. Combine the sherry, butter, and shortening in a medium saucepan and stir over medium heat for 1 minute. Add the cinnamon, the lemon zest, and salt; stir. Add 2¹/₄ cups flour and the seasoned olive oil and stir quickly. Remove from heat and continue stirring for 5 minutes. A dough should be forming. Knead the dough on a floured surface for 2 minutes. Form into a ball and let rest for 1 hour.

Roll into a large ¹/₄-inch-thick sheet; then cut the sheet of dough into about 20 (3-inch) triangles. Heat 4 cups olive oil in a heavy-bottomed pan to about 350 degrees. Deep-fry dough triangles in batches for about 2 minutes per side. Transfer to paper towels to absorb some oil. Serve pastries on a platter drizzled with orange-honey glaze and more sesame seeds.

For the orange glaze: Combine ingredients in a small saucepan and cook on low heat for 15 minutes. Cool to room temperature and use as sauce for the pestinos.

Polverones

Spanish Almond Cookies

Take a double batch to the next fiesta you are invited to and you're sure to be invited back.

Makes 20 small cookies

1 1/2 cups unbleached white flour

3/4 cup raw almonds

1/2 cup plus 2 tablespoons
   butter or margarine

3/4 cup granulated sugar

1/2 teaspoon cinnamon

Powdered sugar for dusting

Preheat the oven to 350 degrees. Measure and pour flour out onto a cookie sheet. Place in oven and "toast" the flour. Occasionally move the flour around on the sheet so that it toasts evenly. Leave in oven for about 8 minutes. Remove and set aside. Place raw almonds on another cookie sheet and toast until they change color just slightly. Remove and place almonds in a food processor. Process almonds until they are finely ground.

Reduce oven temperature to 250 degrees. Place remaining ingredients except dusting sugar in the food processor with the almonds and mix for 20 seconds. Remove and form into a ball. Divide the ball into 20 small pieces and roll them into small 2-inch logs. Cook on a sheet pan for 30 minutes. Remove from oven and cool to room temperature. Dust generously with powdered sugar and serve on a platter.

Magdalenas

Sweet Spanish Cakes

These little cakes are popular for weekend brunches with a cup of café con leche.

Makes 16

1 cup sugar, divided

4 eggs

4 tablespoons butter

Zest of 1 lemon

1 tablespoon milk

1⅔ cups flour

1 teaspoon baking powder

Preheat the oven to 375 degrees. Measure ¼ cup sugar into a small bowl and reserve. In a medium-size mixing bowl, beat the eggs with ¾ cup sugar until the mixture is light. Melt the butter on medium heat in a saucepan or in the microwave. Make sure that the butter cools slightly and is not bubbling. As you continue to beat the egg mixture, slowly pour in the melted butter, making sure to mix thoroughly. Stir in the lemon zest and milk.

Measure out the flour into a separate bowl; add the baking powder and combine thoroughly. While stirring the egg mixture, add in the flour mixture. Continue to stir until all ingredients are mixed well. The batter will be very thick.

Place paper liners in a cupcake or muffin tin. Fill each liner half full with batter. (The batter will more than double in size when baked.) Use a teaspoon to sprinkle each Magdalena with a bit of the reserved sugar. Place pans on the middle shelf of the preheated oven and cook for 18–20 minutes, until Magdalenas have turned golden. Remove from oven; allow to cool for 5 minutes before taking out of the pan to cool further.

Tarta de Higos
Almond Fig Tart

At La Boca Restaurant in Santa Fe, this one always gets rave reviews.

Makes 2 (8-inch) tarts

Tart Dough

1¼ cups flour plus extra for
   dusting the work surface

½ teaspoon salt

2 tablespoons sugar

10 tablespoons cold unsalted butter

1 egg

4 tablespoons cold water

Fig Filling

3 cups dried figs

1 teaspoon ground cardamom

2 teaspoons freshly grated gingerroot

½ cup oloroso sherry

Zest of 1 orange

¼ cup brown sugar

Almond Topping

2 eggs

¼ cup sugar

2 tablespoons butter

1 cup almond paste

For the tart dough: Mix the flour, salt, and sugar together in a bowl. Cut in the butter with a pastry knife and mix well. Add the egg and mix well. Add the cold water and mix with your hands until a dough ball is formed. Wrap the dough ball in plastic wrap and chill for 30 minutes.

Roll out the dough on a floured work surface to about ¼-inch thickness. Divide between two 8-inch tart pans.

For the fig filling: Heat the figs, cardamom, gingerroot, and sherry together on low heat for 15 minutes. Transfer to a food processor and blend with the zest and sugar. Set aside.

For the almond topping: Blend eggs and sugar together in a food processor. Blend in the butter and almond paste. Set this mixture aside.

To assemble: Heat oven to 350 degrees. Spread fig filling onto tart dough in the pans. Top with the almond paste topping, spreading it evenly. Bake for 25 minutes. Allow to cool to room temperature.

Crema de Limon

Lemon Cream

You won't even have to turn on the oven to make this cool and refreshing chilled cream. This is a great one to have the kids help prepare.

Serves 4

6 ounces sweetened condensed milk

6 ounces fresh lemon juice

2 cups plain yogurt

Zest of 1 lemon

1 tablespoon chopped mint

Use a stick blender or a food processor. Combine the condensed milk and lemon juice and mix well. Add half of the yogurt and mix well. Add the other half and mix well. Chill this mixture for 1 hour. Serve in 4 small bowls and garnish with zest and mint.

Flan de Café

Coffee Custard

Flan should always be cooked in a water bath for a gentler way to bring the mixture to high temperature. This prevents cooking the eggs too hard and fast, thus avoiding a scrambled-eggs look. The flan should have a nice smooth texture with this method.

Serves 6

¾ cup sugar, divided

¾ cup lowfat milk

¾ cup whipping cream

20 whole coffee beans

½ cup espresso coffee

3 eggs

1 teaspoon vanilla extract

Wipe out the ramekins to ensure that there is no dust in them. Set in a, 9 x 13-inch glass baking dish. Heat 4–5 cups of water in a pot for the water bath.

Put a heavy skillet or saucepan over medium heat for 30 seconds. Add ½ cup sugar. With the back of a wooden spoon, keep sugar moving constantly until it is completely melted and caramelized (rich medium brown color). Carefully spoon caramelized sugar into each of the 6 ramekins and tip the dishes so the syrup coats the bottoms. Do this quickly, as the syrup will harden fast.

Preheat oven to 325 degrees. Scald the milk and cream along with the coffee beans by heating in a saucepan to just below the boiling point. (Keep a close eye on the pan so it does not boil.). Remove immediately and stir in the coffee.

Meanwhile. in a mixing bowl, beat the eggs slightly. Mix in remaining ¼ cup sugar. Stirring constantly, gradually add hot cream mixture to egg yolk mixture. Stir until the sugar is dissolved. Blend in vanilla extract.

Ladle mixture into ramekins. Carefully remove 1 or 2 ramekins to provide some room to pour. Pour hot water around the ramekins until there is about $^1/_2$ inch of water in the 9 x 13-inch baking dish. Replace ramekins. If the water level does not reach three-fourths of the way up the sides of the ramekins, carefully add more water. Bake uncovered in water bath for 50–60 minutes, or until a knife inserted halfway between the center and edge of a dish comes out clean. Note: To ensure the custard does not overcook, check doneness after 45 minutes, then every 3–5 minutes.

Carefully remove each ramekin from the water bath. Set on a cooling rack until lukewarm, then chill thoroughly in refrigerator. This usually takes at least 1 hour. When ready to serve, unmold by running a knife around the inside edge of baking dish. Place a small dessert plate on the top of the ramekin. With one hand under the ramekin and the other on top of the plate, turn over. Tap the ramekin and the flan should drop onto the plate. If it does not, carefully "prod" the flan out of the ramekin with a small paring knife. Some of the caramelized sugar will have liquefied to a sauce.

Index

Metric Conversion Chart

Volume Measurements		Weight Measurements		Temperature Conversion	
U.S.	METRIC	U.S.	METRIC	FAHRENHEIT	CELSIUS
1 teaspoon	5 ml	½ ounce	15 g	250	120
1 tablespoon	15 ml	1 ounce	30 g	300	150
¼ cup	60 ml	3 ounces	90 g	325	160
⅓ cup	75 ml	4 ounces	115 g	350	180
½ cup	125 ml	8 ounces	225 g	375	190
⅔ cup	150 ml	12 ounces	350 g	400	200
¾ cup	175 ml	1 pound	450 g	425	220
1 cup	250 ml	2¼ pounds	1 kg	450	230